PRAISE FOR *THE 5 LANGUAGES OF APPRECIATION IN THE WORKPLACE*

After twenty years of coaching leaders at all levels, and educating thousands of professional coaches around the world, I believe there are two universal things that ignite excellence within people: recognition of their uniqueness and acknowledgement that they matter. *The 5 Languages of Appreciation in the Workplace* gives individuals, teams, and entire organizations an invaluable resource to do just that by making appreciation a foundational part of their culture.

AMY RUPPERT, Master Certified Coach; CEO, The Integreship Group; Past National President, the International Coaching Federation

Good leaders are known for their technical skills. Great leaders are known and remembered for how they make people feel. *The 5 Languages of Appreciation in the Workplace* is a must-have resource for any leader who wants to move the bar from being a good leader to a great leader.

KAREN ALBER, Founding Partner, The Integreship Group; Former Chief Information Officer, HJ Heinz

The 5 Languages of Appreciation in the Workplace has helped change the way managers around the world think about appreciation in the workplace. New research on the positive benefits to organizations when employees feel valued and appreciated for their contributions, generational differences, the special needs of remote employees, and peer-to-peer appreciation, are welcomed additions to a book that has already become a management classic. This book will be equally valuable to those who are at the start of their burgeoning management careers as it will be to seasoned managers by providing practical tips on how to engage the increasingly diverse workforce with relevant and relatable solutions.

PETER HART, President & CEO, Rideau, Inc.; Director, Advisory Board, Wharton Center for Human Resources, University of Pennsylvania

The 5 Languages of Appreciation in the Workplace has been a pivotal resource helping our employees and culture grow and mature. It is amazing to see how trust grows when care and appreciation are shown, as the correct language of appreciation for each employee is utilized. The insights found in this book are applicable to all generations and skill sets: introverts to extroverts, technical to relational abilities—all have been able to apply these principles for meaningful growth.

EVAN WILSON, Chief Experience Officer, Meritrust Credit Union

There is a continual cry for authenticity in our workplaces and communities. This updated version of *The 5 Languages of Appreciation in the Workplace* brings a deeper understanding of HOW to be authentic in expressing individual value in a variety of circumstances. The business case for adopting *The 5 Languages of Appreciation* is stronger than ever, and this new edition provides the research foundation for the return on investment to organizations when they commit to building a strong, positive workplace culture, one coworker at a time!

DAN AGNE, Owner and Principal Consultant, The Agne Group; Director of Sales Effectiveness, The Brooks Group; Associate Pastor, Open Bible Christian Church, Dayton, Ohio

I greatly appreciate this second edition of *The 5 Languages of Appreciation in the Workplace*. White and Chapman have done an exceptional job of mixing statistics with stories and infusing research into relevancy. They give readers a nuanced approach to appreciating others at work that will enhance leaders' and colleagues' appreciation-literacy skills in being able to draw out the best in others at work (and home).

DAVID ZINGER, Founder, The Global Employee Experience & Engagement Network; Coauthor, *People Artists: Drawing Out the Best in Others at Work*

Drs. Chapman and White's perspective about the reality of managers' lives is spot on. Managers don't have capacity to give as much appreciation as the human spirit of their direct reports craves, in most cases. "It takes a village to raise a child" applies just as much to nurturing the fundamental needs of all human beings to be understood, valued, and appreciated. We all live, to some degree, in a "village" community and the principles in *The 5 Languages of Appreciation in the Workplace* make it much easier to do what most people intuitively want to give and receive.

TIM MYERS, Materials Lab Manager-Metallography, Honeywell, Inc.

Appreciation isn't just a manager issue; it is a coworker issue. It is an employee appreciating their leader issue, and a vendor to employee issue—the list goes on and on. In *The 5 Languages of Appreciation in the Workplace*, Drs. Chapman and White give us the vision to create a culture with everyone valuing and appreciating one another no matter the role they have in the organization.

TIFFANY SNIPES, Learning & Development Consultant, BJC Institute for Learning and Development

As a longtime user of the *5 Languages* approach, I was excited to see the new material that has been added to highlight the proven financial benefits of appreciation, working with remote and virtual teams, appreciation across generations, and making a strong case for the overall increase in employee engagement. We continue to offer training on *The 5 Languages of Appreciation in the Workplace* as a valuable tool to our member companies. We have found that when team members learn what others actually value in regards to showing appreciation to each other, areas like team morale, cohesiveness, unity, and especially productivity increase, and drama decreases.

DAVE TIPPETT, Director, On Site Learning and Consulting, The Employers' Association

Understanding *The 5 Languages of Appreciation in the Workplace* has been critical to our success in building a strong team and maintaining a positive culture. I aspire daily to demonstrate authentic appreciation toward my team members, peers, and leadership team. The focus on appreciation has increased employee engagement and strengthened our team dynamic.

MICHELLE SUTTER, Director of Sales, Holland America Line

Working with Dr. White brought to light the importance of building a sustainable appreciation culture. Through his workshops and personalized recognition tools, we are starting to see improved team dynamics and our appreciation communication shifting in the direction of tomorrow. While it didn't come naturally at first, we are learning to recognize each other's language of appreciation and it is making a big difference.

JOANNA ZIARNIK, Research & Innovation, L'Oreal USA

THE
5 LANGUAGES
OF
APPRECIATION
IN THE
WORKPLACE

EMPOWERING ORGANIZATIONS BY
ENCOURAGING PEOPLE

Gary Chapman
& Paul White

NORTHFIELD PUBLISHING

CHICAGO

Edited by Elizabeth Cody Newenhuyse
Interior design: Erik M. Peterson
Cover design: Faceout Studio
Gary Chapman photo: P.S. Photography
Paul White photo: Michael Bankston

Some names and details have been changed to protect the privacy of individuals.

The Library of Congress has cataloged the first printing of this book as follows:
Chapman, Gary D. The 5 languages of appreciation in the workplace :
empowering organizations by encouraging people / Gary D. Chapman and Paul E. White.
p. cm.
Includes bibliographical references.
ISBN 978-0-8024-6176-6
1. Employee motivation. 2. Personnel management. I. White, Paul E.,
II. Title. III. Title: Five languages of appreciation in the workplace. HF5549.5.M63C438 2011
658.3'14--dc22
2011004614

ISBN: 978-0-8024-1840-1

All websites and phone numbers listed herein are accurate at the time of publication but may change in the future or cease to exist. The listing of website references and resources does not imply publisher endorsement of the site's entire contents. Groups and organizations are listed for informational purposes, and listing does not imply publisher endorsement of their activities.

We hope you enjoy this book from Northfield Publishing. Our goal is to provide high-quality, thought-provoking books and products that connect truth to your real needs and challenges. For more information on other books and products that will help you with all your important relationships, go to northfieldpublishing.com or write to:

Northfield Publishing
820 N. LaSalle Boulevard
Chicago, IL 60610

3 5 7 9 10 8 6 4 2

Printed in the United States of America

Dedicated to our parents,
Sam and Grace Chapman
and
Roger and Eleanor White,
who modeled hard work and perseverance
throughout their lives—
without always receiving much appreciation
while doing so

CONTENTS

Preface to the Updated Edition 9

Introduction 11

1. What Employees Want Most 17

2. For Business Leaders: Why Appreciation Is a Good
   Investment 27

3. Appreciation: From Both Managers and Peers 47

4. Appreciation Language #1: Words of Affirmation 55

5. Appreciation Language #2: Quality Time 67

6. Appreciation Language #3: Acts of Service 81

7. Appreciation Language #4: Tangible Gifts 93

8. Appreciation Language #5: Physical Touch 105

9. Discover Your Primary Appreciation Language:
   The MBA Inventory 117

10. The Difference between Recognition and Appreciation 129

11. Your Potential Blind Spot: Your Least Valued Language 141

12. Appreciation with Remote Employees and Virtual Teams 151

13. Generational Differences and Other FAQs 167

14. How Appreciation Works in Different Settings 183

15. Does a Person's Language of Appreciation Ever Change? 195

16. Overcoming Your Challenges 207

17. What If You Don't Appreciate Your Team Members? 223

18. Now It's Your Turn 233

Notes 241

About the Authors 251

PREFACE TO THE UPDATED EDITION

IN 2009, WE BEGAN RESEARCHING how the five love languages might apply to work-based relationships, focusing on "appreciation" as the parallel concept in the workplace. We developed the *Motivating By Appreciation (MBA) Inventory* to help gather information to help in this process. We also created a range of *Appreciation at Work* resources to assist leaders and trainers in applying the concept of authentic appreciation with their managers, supervisors, and employees.

Since 2011, when *The 5 Languages of Appreciation in the Workplace* was originally published, the response has been exciting. We have sold over 300,000 copies of the book in English, and over 150,000 individuals have taken the online *MBA Inventory* to identify their primary, secondary, and least valued languages of appreciation. Our book has been translated into seventeen languages and our materials have been used in at least sixty countries. We have over 700 certified facilitators of our *Appreciation at Work* workshop across the globe. And most importantly, the sales and reach of our book continue to grow each year (selling over 40,000 copies each year)—helping leaders and employees throughout the world learn how to communicate appreciation effectively to their team members.

The concept of appreciation in the workplace remains highly relevant to developing positive workplace environments, and at every level of an organization individual employees strongly desire to be appreciated. But the workplace continues to change, and we have learned much over the past decade in understanding important factors to communicating authentic appreciation across a wide range of work settings.

As a result, our goals for the updated, revised version of *The 5 Languages of Appreciation in the Workplace* are to:

- cite recent research related to appreciation;
- share important lessons learned from the thousands of employees with whom we have worked;
- provide examples from a wide range of industries;
- clarify points that we feel are critical to understanding and applying the 5 languages of appreciation practically;
- connect you with the numerous resources (articles, videos, podcasts, assessment tools, training materials, visual symbols) we've created to help you build workplace cultures of appreciation.

We trust this updated version will be a valuable resource to those who previously read the first edition, and also to those who are just learning about the power of communicating authentic appreciation to help workplace relationships become healthier and more positive.

Warmly,
PAUL WHITE, PhD
GARY CHAPMAN, PhD

INTRODUCTION

DO YOU FEEL APPRECIATED by the people you work with? If so, then you probably enjoy going to work each day. However, if you do not feel appreciated, then your work may simply be a means of keeping food on the table. All of us expect to get paid for the work we do. Yes, we would all like to make more money. But the number one factor in job satisfaction is not the amount of pay we receive but whether or not we feel appreciated and valued for the work we do. A new survey by the Society of Human Resource Management shows that employee recognition and engagement are key to retaining good employees. And, according to research conducted by the US Department of Labor, 64% of Americans who leave their jobs say they do so because they don't feel appreciated.[1]

This is true of employees across the board, from CEOs to housekeeping staff. Something deep within the human psyche cries out for appreciation. When that need is unmet, then an employee's level of engagement with their work will be low.

Here are the comments of three employees who work in very different settings—but share a desire to feel appreciated.

"IT'S NOT ABOUT MONEY"

"I would not be leaving if I just knew that they valued the work I do," Dave said. Dave was a thirty-year-old assistant to the CFO of a commercial real estate firm. He had been working for the firm for about fifteen months and initially was excited about the opportunity the position gave him for personal and professional growth. But over time, he grew more and more disillusioned.

Dave informed us he had resigned from his current accounting position and was moving to a different firm. "It's not about money. It's just that no matter what I do—how long I work or what I accomplish—I never hear anything positive. If I make a mistake, I hear about it immediately, but if I do my job well, the silence is overwhelming."

* * * * *

In a session we were conducting with the staff of a successful manufacturing company, Cindy laughed and said, "That'll be the day!" We were discussing the results of the *MBA Inventory* with the team. Cindy's primary language of appreciation is acts of service. Cindy, the executive assistant to the patriarch and CEO of a family-owned business, loves it when coworkers pitch in and help her get tasks done, especially when the workload is heavy. She had worked for Mr. Stevens for over twenty years and knew him as well as anyone. Even though the CEO, now in his seventies, only worked part-time, Cindy still had plenty of work to do—planning his extensive travel, managing his personal affairs, and keeping him up-to-date on how the business was doing.

Cindy indicated in her *MBA Inventory* results that if her colleagues (or supervisor) wanted to show their appreciation for her, they could help her get her work done if she was feeling overwhelmed. She said, "If Mr. Stevens lifted one finger to help me get something done, I'd fall over and die from a heart attack." She was joking—but there clearly was an edge to her response.

* * * * *

"I love working here," Elena said. "I can't think of any other place I would rather work than for Dr. Jones. Now, don't get me wrong. Dr. Jones is demanding. He expects you to do your work well. We work hard, see a lot of patients, and we are all held accountable for getting our tasks completed with the highest level of quality care for our patients." We had heard from other sources that Dr. Jones, an optometrist, worked hard and efficiently, and provided excellent care for his patients. And we had heard that medical assistants were lined up waiting to work for him.

Why? "Because Dr. Jones treats us so well. He's always doing things to make sure that we feel cared for."

For example: "Once a month he orders in lunch for the staff (we take an extra half hour for these lunches). We have a staff meeting where we discuss what's going on in the office—what is working well, and areas that are creating challenges for us—and we discuss how to make things go better. Sometimes he will share new research or new techniques in the field with us during this time.

"And at Christmastime he gives us a paid day to go shopping and gives us a hundred-dollar gift card to use. But most of all, he is positive and encouraging to us. He frequently tells us that we are doing a good job—both individually and as a team. You couldn't get me to go work for any other office, no matter how much you paid me."

THE 5 LOVE LANGUAGES® GOES TO WORK

As these real-life examples show, what makes one person feel appreciated does not necessarily make another person feel appreciated. Thus, even in companies where recognition is deemed important, efforts at expressing appreciation are often ineffective. As a result of the significant impact *The 5 Love Languages®* has had on millions of personal relationships and the critical importance that effective communication of appreciation and encouragement has in the workplace, we are committed to providing the resources to help you apply these concepts to better understand—and appreciate—those with whom you work. To keep from overburdening the casual reader but at the same time let the more deeply interested explore this additional information, we have provided links to videos, articles, and resources developed by means of numerical references in each chapter. These can be referenced in the **Notes** section at the end of the book.

Let's get started by looking further at just why appreciation in the workplace is so important to the health of your employees—and your business.

CHAPTER 1

WHAT EMPLOYEES WANT MOST

I (GARY) WAS HAVING DINNER with a friend who is on staff at a large nonprofit organization. I was giving him a brief overview of the research Dr. White and I were doing with the *Appreciation at Work* resources we had developed. When I finished I said, "Could I ask you a personal question about your own work?" "Certainly," he said.

I continued, "On a scale of 0–10, how appreciated do you feel by your immediate supervisor?" "About 5," he said. I could detect a tinge of disappointment in his voice.

My second question followed. "On a scale of 0–10, how appreciated do you feel by your coworkers?" "About an 8," he said. "How many people work closely with you?" I inquired. "Two," he responded. "Do you feel equally appreciated by the two of them?" I asked. "No," he said. "One would be a 6 and the other a 9. That's why I said about an 8."

Whether you are a business owner, CEO, supervisor, or a co-worker, this book is designed to help you learn how to communicate appreciation in ways that are meaningful to the individuals with whom you work. One exciting lesson we have learned: *Anyone can make a difference in their workplace, regardless of their position*—whether supervisors, coworkers, receptionists, managers, frontline employees, or team members from other departments.

Why is feeling appreciated so important in a work setting? Because each of us wants to know that what we are doing matters. Without a sense of being valued by supervisors and colleagues, workers start to feel like a machine or a commodity. If no one notices a person's commitment to doing the job well, that person's motivation tends to wane over time. Steven Covey, author of the bestselling *The 7 Habits of Highly Effective People*, felt so strongly about people's need for appreciation that he stated: "Next to physical survival, the greatest need of a human being is psychological survival, to be understood, to be affirmed, to be validated, to be appreciated."[1]

> Anyone can make a difference in their workplace, regardless of their position.

When individuals do not feel truly valued and appreciated, the results are predictable:

- Workers become discouraged, feeling: "There's always more to do and no one notices or cares about the contribution I make."

- Employees become more negative about their work with increasing grumbling, complaining, and gossiping.

- Tardiness (at the beginning of the day, from breaks, after lunch) increases, as does the rate of employees calling in "sick."

- Team members will experience a lack of connectedness with others and with the mission of the organization (and, as a result, employee engagement ratings decline).

- Eventually, team members start to consider leaving the organization, they begin to search for other employment, and staff turnover increases.

WHY "JUST SAY THANKS" DOESN'T WORK

Communicating appreciation to employees and colleagues sounds pretty easy and straightforward. In many ways, it is. However, we also know that for the communication of appreciation to effectively encourage the other person, several factors must be considered.

First, researchers have found that attempts to communicate appreciation globally across an organization are not very effective. One employee said of his organization, "We're pretty good at showing recognition company-wide. But I don't think we do a good job of it individually." Trying a general "just say thanks" campaign across the company will not have much impact and can actually backfire, sparking cynicism in the ranks. While we all want to know that we are valued, we want it to be authentic, not contrived.

Here are some other differences between recognition and appreciation:

Recognition is largely about behavior. "Catch them doing what you want and recognize it," the books say. Appreciation, conversely, focuses not only on performance but also affirms the employee's value as a person.

Recognition is about improving performance and focuses on what is good for the company. Appreciation emphasizes what

Appreciation emphasizes what is good for the company and good for the person. is good for the company and good for the person (which may sometimes mean helping them find a position that is better for them than their current role).

Recognition requires only that you implement certain behaviors: defining desired behaviors, monitoring them, and rewarding them when they occur. Authentic appreciation involves both behavior and heart attitude. Have you ever received "appreciation" from someone and you seriously questioned its genuineness? Trying to "fake" appreciating someone doesn't work well.

Finally, the relational direction of recognition is top-down, coming from supervisors, managers, or the HR department. Appreciation, on the other hand, can be communicated in any direction—from colleague to colleague, from supervisor to team member, or even from a frontline worker to the president of the company.

HITTING THE BULL'S-EYE VS. MISSING THE MARK ALTOGETHER

But the challenge, from a supervisor's (or coworker's) perspective, is to know what actions hit the mark and effectively communicate appreciation to a team member. This is why we developed the *Motivating By Appreciation Inventory*,[2] which includes specific "action items" for each language of appreciation. We wanted to develop a tool that provided accurate, individualized actions business owners and organizational leaders can use to show their appreciation for their team members without having to guess about what will be most significant to the employee. We agree with Buckingham and Clifton who state in their bestselling book, *Now, Discover Your Strengths*: "To excel as a manager, to turn your people's talents into productive powerful strengths, requires an additional, all-important ingredient. Lacking this ingredient . . . you will never reach excellence. The all-important ingredient is *Individualization*."[3]

We have found many organizations are looking for ways to encourage their team members and reward them for work well done, but using financial rewards to accomplish this purpose is not realistic. This is especially true in the areas of government, schools, social service agencies, ministries, and nonprofit organizations. Directors and administrators must find ways to encourage team members that do not require large amounts of financial resources. (In reality, as is discussed in the following chapter, using financial rewards to motivate and show appreciation is not very effective.)

Finally, there is a bit of good news for organizational leaders. When leaders actively pursue teaching their team members how to communicate authentic appreciation in the ways desired by the recipients, the whole work culture improves. Interestingly, even managers and supervisors report they enjoy their work more! *All* of us thrive in an atmosphere of appreciation.

WHEN APPRECIATION MISSES THE MARK

We have found that each person has a primary and secondary language of appreciation. Our primary language communicates more deeply to us than the others. Although we will accept appreciation in all five languages, we will not *feel* truly valued unless the message is communicated through our primary language. When messages are repeatedly sent in ways outside of that language, the intent of the message "misses the mark" and loses the impact the sender had hoped for.

We all tend to communicate to others in ways that are most meaningful to us—we "speak our own language." However, if the message is not expressed in the appreciation language of the intended recipient, the action will not be especially meaningful to them. That is why many employees are not encouraged when they receive a reward as part of the company's recognition plan— it doesn't speak in their preferred language of appreciation. (Or, even if their language is Tangible Gifts, the specific reward may not have much value to them.)

"I've gotten various gifts over the years for anniversaries or recognition for 'above and beyond' effort," said one woman who works in a midsized company. "But since gifts are my least-favored language, these don't do a lot for me. You know what makes me feel good? Having a really interesting conversation with my boss or other senior leaders about what's going on in the organization." This woman's primary language of appreciation is Quality Time. For her, trinkets miss the mark.

Then there's Lindsay, who consistently leads her department in sales and has the highest marks in customer service. At their department's quarterly meetings, she is regularly called forward to receive a reward. For Lindsay, this is like torture. She hates to be in front of groups, and she doesn't want public attention. What she would value is time with her supervisor regularly where she could share her ideas on how to improve customer service. Lindsay's primary language of appreciation is also Quality Time, not Words of Affirmation. Giving her public recognition is embarrassing to Lindsay and a negative experience for her— clearly not affirming.

This process of miscommunication can be frustrating to both the sender and the recipient. Consider the following scenario:

"What's the matter with Elliot?" Anna asked a colleague. "I tell him he's doing a good job. I even bought him tickets to the Lakers game this weekend to show him how much I appreciated the extra hours he put in to get the project done. And yet, he mopes around here and tells Alex that he doesn't feel the management team really values what he does. What does he want?"

What Elliot wants is help from his teammates when a project needs to be done. He doesn't like to work by himself, although he will if necessary. He values Acts of Service and would be really encouraged if either his colleagues or his supervisor would stay late with him some evening and pitch in to help him get the project done. Telling him "Thanks" or giving him some tangible gift after the fact is okay, but it doesn't really meet his emotional need for feeling appreciated.

This leads to the overall thesis of this book. *We believe that people in the workplace need to feel appreciated in order for them to enjoy their job, do their best work, and continue working over the long haul.* When team members feel truly valued, good results follow.

Tony Schwartz, president and CEO of The Energy Project, puts it well:

> Whatever else each of us derives from our work, there may be nothing more precious than the feeling that we truly matter—that we contribute unique value to the whole, and that we're recognized for it.
>
> The single highest driver of engagement, according to a worldwide study conducted by Towers Watson, is whether or not workers feel their managers are genuinely interested in their wellbeing.[4]

Understanding what makes you and your coworkers feel encouraged can significantly improve your relationships in the workplace, increase team members' sense of engagement, and create a more positive work environment. Our goal is to provide the tools, resources, and information to help you gather this knowledge and apply it in a practical, meaningful way in your work setting.

Making It Personal

1. When you want to communicate appreciation to your colleagues, how do you typically do so? How effective do you believe your actions are (in making your colleague feel appreciated)?

2. How well do you believe your coworkers know how to express appreciation to you? What have they tried? What has been the impact on you?

3. When you feel discouraged at work, what actions by others can encourage you?

4. On a scale of 1–10, how appreciated do you currently feel by your immediate supervisor?

5. On a scale of 1–10, how appreciated do you feel by your coworkers?

CHAPTER 2

FOR BUSINESS LEADERS:

WHY APPRECIATION IS A GOOD INVESTMENT

THE PRIMARY PURPOSE OF a business is to provide valued goods and services in ways that meet the customers' needs and desires and allow the company to make a profit while doing so (as well as having a positive impact on its community and other stakeholders). As a result, business leaders strongly focus on the profitability of the business and the return on investment (ROI) being produced for the owners. In fact, ROI is one of the measuring sticks by which executives and managers are monitored regarding their professional performance.

While most owners want their staff to enjoy their work and have positive attitudes about the company, the majority of leaders assess the benefits of any program or activity in terms of its impact on the financial health of the company. If an activity does not add to the health of the company and, at the same time, takes away employees' focus and energy, why would a manager want to try it?

Often when we share about our *Appreciation at Work* resources with business executives and organizational leaders, ultimately the question "Why?" arises. "Why should we be concerned about communicating appreciation to our employees? We pay them fairly. In light of the challenges from the global economy, they should be thankful they have a job. Yes, I want them to be happy and feel appreciated; but, on the other hand, we're running a business here. This is not about hugs and warm fuzzies; it is about providing goods and services while making a profit."

> A reality-based question that needs to be answered is: "What benefits will I or my organization gain from training my leaders and staff in communicating authentic appreciation to one another?"

This response is neither unusual nor unreasonable for those who are responsible for the financial well-being of a business. The world of work is a demanding environment with harsh realities. Managers and directors have to deal with global competition, reduced budgets, increased taxes, and often an untrained workforce. No one has extra time or energy to waste on projects that do not contribute to the success of the organization. So, a reality-based question that needs to be answered is: "What benefits will I (or my organization) gain from training my leaders and staff in communicating authentic appreciation to one another?"

MISCONCEPTIONS LEADERS HOLD
ABOUT APPRECIATION

Before we show the reasons why training team members to com-municate authentic appreciation is beneficial to organizations and their employees, we must first address some mistaken beliefs some leaders have, so they can clearly "hear" the compelling evidence supporting the value of appreciation and encouragement.

One false assumption is that *the primary goal of communicating appreciation is to make employees feel good.* This belief often seems to be held by individuals on the cynical side, who disparagingly condemn all appreciation as being "touchy-feely" and worthless. A common mantra is: "Work is about getting things done. I don't care how people feel about it."

Unfortunately, there is some basis for holding this belief. In the world of encouragement and positive thinking, some well-meaning individuals have taken the appreciation emphasis to the extreme of having a goal of "making everyone happy." As professional counselors, we can easily assert that this is, and will be, a failing endeavor. Why? Because no one can make someone else happy.

Even if our focus is narrowed to helping people "feel good," attaining this goal will also fail. We know that our feeling responses are essentially a result of whether our expectations are met in real life. If they are met, we are pleased; if they are not met, we become frustrated, angry, or disappointed. Although we can assist people in learning to adjust their expectations more closely to reality, no one can make anyone else feel anything.

A second misconception held by many leaders is that *certain types of career groups and occupations are more receptive to the concept of communicating appreciation than other industries are.* In fact, our experience has found this *not* to be the case: the issue is less about the industry or work setting and more about the organizational leader or supervisor.

We gathered a list of professions, occupations, and work settings in which research has been published regarding the importance of appreciation in the workplace. Please note that this is *not* an exhaustive list—partly because there is new research being published virtually every month.

Senior living care providers	Paralegals / legal assistants	Medical group administrators
Bank employees	Social workers	Dentists
Public school teachers	Accountants	Day spa managers
Optometrists	Child care providers	Veterinarians
Manufacturing line workers	Government agency employees	Customer service representatives
Industrial workers	Nurses	Educational administrators
Home health providers	College & university staff	Military personnel
Remote employees	IT professionals	Insurance agency staff
Law enforcement officers	Hotel staff	Restaurant employees

Obviously, the variety of occupations and industries that have been shown to be affected by the communication of appreciation in the workplace is vast. And the issue is not limited to North America—we have worked with multinational companies and businesses throughout Europe, Asia, Africa, South America, and Australia and found that communication of appreciation in the workplace has a positive impact on organizational health.[1]

THE BENEFITS OF APPRECIATION

When determining the positive results of any process or product, there are three primary sources of information to examine:

1. Research-based evidence,
2. Individual testimonies and stories, and
3. The response in the marketplace over time.

The most compelling argument for the value of a product would be to have corroborative positive results from all three sources. Let's examine these.

Research-based evidence

Because the volume of research is so large (and continually growing), we have chosen to summarize the findings and reference the source for those who want to explore the research more deeply. For context, we have developed a flowchart linking appreciation in the workplace to positive work outcomes (see next page).

Appreciation in the workplace is directly related to employee engagement. The degree to which employees feel appreciated is one of the core factors the Gallup researchers found to significantly impact the level of employee engagement in organizations.[2] A Glassdoor survey found four out of five employees (81%) say they are "motivated to work harder when their boss shows appreciation for their work."[3] Forbes recommends demonstrating appreciation for employees' contributions as a means to increase employee engagement.[4] Employee engagement has been found to be three times more strongly related to intrinsic motivators than extrinsic rewards,[5] and intrinsic motivation is a stronger predictor of job performance than extrinsic rewards.[6]

THE IMPORTANCE OF EMPLOYEE ENGAGEMENT

Over several years the Gallup organization conducted research and interviews with one million employees across the world, identifying the core factors that contribute to increasing employee engagement in workplaces.[7] Employee engagement has been defined as "the emotional commitment the employee has to the organization and its goals." This emotional commitment means "engaged employees actually *care* about their work and their company."[8]

The level of employee engagement within a workplace is important to leaders because it has been shown to be highly predictive of numerous positive benefits that impact the functioning and financial viability of a company.[9]

CHART 1

The Overall Impact of Employee Engagement on Organizations

Result of Employee Engagement	Research Findings
Employees show up for work	Engaged employees average 27% fewer days missed than those who are highly disengaged.
Less staff turnover	Business groups with more disengaged employees have 51% more turnover than business units with more engaged workers.
Fewer employee accidents on the job	On-the-job accidents are 62% more likely in companies with high levels of disengagement in comparison to businesses with more engaged employees.
Less employee theft	Companies that have high levels of disengagement lose 51% more of their inventory than companies with a highly engaged workforce.
Higher customer ratings	Companies with higher levels of employee engagement have 12% higher customer rating scores than those with low employee engagement.
Greater productivity	Companies in the top 25% of employee engagement averaged 18% higher productivity than the companies in the bottom 25%.
Increased profitability	In a meta-analysis of 263 research studies, employers with the most engaged employees were 22% more profitable than those with the least engaged employees.[10]

APPRECIATION AND RECOGNITION
LINKED TO POSITIVE OUTCOMES

In addition to the positive results from overall employee engagement, researchers have also found these specific findings directly related to communicating appreciation, recognition, and praise to employees:[11]

- Improving the levels of praise and recognition received by employees was found to *increase productivity and revenue between 10–20%.*

- Increasing the frequency of recognition and praise was found to *increase patients' ratings of their experience at one large medical facility by 11%.*

- When comparing 60 different business teams, *the highest-performing teams had 5.6 times more positive comments than negative remarks.* Conversely, the teams who were the lowest performers had 2.8 negative remarks for every positive comment made.

- *Leaders who give little praise to their team members actually undercut the perceived value of the salaries they are paying.* Employees who report the highest levels of receiving recent recognition are over two times more likely to agree that "from my most objective viewpoint I am paid appropriately for the work I do."

- *Giving praise has been shown to benefit the person who gives the praise*—increasing their level of happiness for up to a month later.

AN ASIDE: MORE MONEY DOESN'T KEEP THEM

When we speak to groups or consult with businesses, we often ask this question: "What do you think is the primary reason people switch jobs?" The most frequent responses received are "for more money" or "to move up—to get a better position." However, we know that leaving for better pay or moving to a higher-level position are not the reasons most people leave their current employment. In fact, research compiled over a four-year time span by one of the leading third-party exit interviewing firms in the United States found the following results from thousands of interviews:

Belief: Most managers (89%) believe employees leave for more money, while only 11% of managers believe employees leave for other reasons.[12]

Fact: In reality, only 12% of employees reported leaving for more money,[13] while 88% of employees state they leave for reasons other than money. In fact, the reasons most often cited by departing employees were more psychological in nature—including not feeling trusted or valued.

The following additional research clarifies the issue even more.

Money: what the studies show

Money isn't an effective motivator for many people. When reviewing over ninety studies over a time span of 120 years, the relationship between salary level and job satisfaction was found to be very weak—how much money employees make accounts for only 2% of the factors contributing to how much they enjoy their work.[14]

- A McKinsey consulting group study found that *monetary rewards are less motivating to employees than nonmonetary incentives.*[15] Praise from the employee's manager, attention from leaders, and the opportunity to lead projects were more motivating and rewarding than financial incentives such as an increase in base salary, bonuses, or stock options.

• Just making more money is not a primary motivator for most baby boomers,[16] Gen Xers,[17] millennials,[18] or those from Generation Z.[19]

• For millennials, the factor reported to have the least impact on increasing personal engagement is "more money."[20]

• In some cases, when financial rewards are increased, the intrinsic motivation (the drive from within a person to complete tasks) of employees actually *decreases*.[21]

• Demonstrating appreciation for employees' contributions increases employee engagement.[22] Employee engagement has been found to be three times more strongly related to intrinsic motivators than extrinsic rewards,[23] and, as we have seen, intrinsic motivation is a stronger predictor of job performance than extrinsic rewards.[24]

Managers and employers need to realize that money isn't a great motivator. Your business or organization is at risk of losing quality team members if your staff doesn't feel appreciated by supervisors and coworkers.[25] Most supervisors are not aware of this fact, and thus they focus more on the power of financial benefits to retain employees. But, as one fed-up manager told us, "They couldn't pay me enough to stay here. The lack of support is overwhelming."

EMPLOYEE TURNOVER: THE ULTIMATE RESULT OF NOT FEELING APPRECIATED

The cost of replacing employees is often cited as the #1 nonproductive cost for businesses and organizations. "Labor turnover is one of the most significant causes of declining productivity and sagging morale in both the public and private sectors."[26]

The cost (overt and hidden) of staff turnover includes the combination of advertising and recruitment of new employees, candidate travel, the costs associated with selection, hiring, assignment, orientation, signing bonuses, and relocation.[27] The cost to the US economy has been estimated to be at least five trillion dollars a year.[28]

For individual organizations the cost of replacing employees has been estimated to be:[29]

- 30–50% of annual salary for an entry-level employee
- 150% of annual salary for mid-level employees
- 400% of annual salary for high-level or highly specialized employees.

The impact of appreciation on staff turnover is dramatic:

- 79% of employees who leave their jobs voluntarily cite a lack of appreciation as a key reason for their leaving.[30]
- 66% of current employees report they would quit if they felt unappreciated.[31]

According to a study by Bersin & Associates, companies that provide ample employee recognition have 31% lower voluntary turnover rates than companies that don't.[32]

The competition for skilled team members is fierce and increasing. As a result, the need to hold onto good employees is one of the most critical tasks of organizational leaders today.[33] In fact, retaining quality employees has been identified by 87% of HR professionals as one of the highest priorities for their profession.[34]

WHAT IS NOT WORKING:
TRADITIONAL EMPLOYEE RECOGNITION

Employee recognition programs have proliferated in the past several years, to the point that 85–90% of businesses in the US have some form of employee recognition program[35] but turnover rates remain high[36] and employee engagement has not increased.[37] Part of this low level of impact has to do with how the programs are structured.[38]

The most common type of recognition is for length of service (96%), followed by retirement recognition (64%);[39] however, these events occur infrequently, and cannot be expected to impact individual work satisfaction or performance on a daily basis.

When recognition is given corporately (from the organization), the most common reward is a trophy, certificate, or plaque (50%), with another 35% being some form of nonmonetary reward (letter or public recognition).[40] While some people certainly beam from being recognized in this manner, others find the public attention embarrassing and makes them feel uncomfortable.[41]

Most incentive-based employee recognition programs (those focusing on performance) emphasize rewards, with companies spending *$90 billion annually* on incentives.[42]

Although rewards are a major emphasis in many recognition programs, only 6% of employees identify tangible gifts as the primary way they want to be shown appreciation.[43]

A national study by the Canadian government concluded: "No matter which type of recognition program organizations have in place, if employees are not being recognized in a way that is valued by them, the recognition is less meaningful."[44]

The unmet desire for appreciation

Feeling appreciated is a strong desire across cultures by virtually all employees, supervisors, managers, and business owners, regardless of work setting. But unfortunately, for most, the need goes unmet:

- In a survey by the *Chicago Tribune* of over 35,000 employees, the *number one* reason cited why they enjoyed their work was: "I feel genuinely appreciated at this company."[45]
- In a global study of over 200,000 employees completed by the Boston Consulting Group, the *most important factor* employees related to enjoying their job was that they felt appreciated (financial compensation didn't show up on the list until #8).[46]
- But 65% of North Americans reported they have received no recognition over the past 12 months.[47]
- In a national Globoforce employee recognition survey across multiple companies, 51% of managers say they do a good job of showing recognition for a job well done. But only 17% of the employees who work for those managers say the manager shows recognition for work well done.[48]
- Expressing appreciation is not a common practice. A study by John Templeton Foundation found that 74% never or rarely express gratitude to their boss, and 60% say they either never express gratitude at work or do so perhaps once a year.[49]
- In a study of over 500,000 employees, PayScale found that "An employee feeling appreciated or unappreciated moves the needle on satisfaction more than any other variable."[50]

The bottom line: authentic appreciation brings positive results to your organization and mitigates the negative consequences that result when employees don't feel valued.

INDIVIDUAL TESTIMONIES AND STORIES

Beyond the research, we can learn a lot from individual stories. While stories and anecdotes shared by individuals do not carry the same weight of influence as "hard-core" data, they still are important. Over the past several years, we have obtained numerous written testimonials (and received innumerable verbal compliments) of the positive impact *The 5 Languages of Appreciation* have had on organizations and leaders across the world. In considering how best to share these, we determined, in the interest of space, we will share a few brief ones and then post more (representing a variety of industries and work settings) on our website at www.appreciationatwork.com/testimonials.

"One of the core strengths for the *Appreciation at Work* process is that it is easily implemented. The resources are adaptable to different settings and roles, able to be used by frontline employees, supervisors, and managers immediately."
—**Andy Bailey, Certified Recognition Professional,**
   Employee Recognition, Events & Corporate Citizenship
   Manager, DIRECTV, LLC

"[*Appreciation at Work*] has combined solid research with actual work-life experiences to show how authentic appreciation positively affects the success and bottom line of an organization."
—**Jack W. Bruce, Past President, SHRM–Atlanta,**
   VP Strategic Operations, The Benefit Company

"*The 5 Languages of Appreciation* dovetails beautifully with other leadership training we've received and provides practical action steps in how to encourage one another."
—**Susan Bukiewicz, Regional Director of Women's Ministries,**
   The Salvation Army

Additionally, the following results are consistently reported to us in our interactions with employees and leaders. When team members learn how to begin to communicate authentic appreciation to one another:

- the quality of relationships improves between workers and their supervisors, and also among coworkers

- attendance improves and productivity increases

- team members are less irritable and internal conflict declines

- the rate of employee turnover decreases

- customer satisfaction ratings rise

- supervisors and managers enjoy their work more

Ultimately, employees state that going to work in an environment where there is a sense of appreciation for what they contribute is more satisfying and enjoyable than doing the same tasks (for the same money) and not feeling valued by those with whom they work. We feel proud and thankful to be able to have a positive effect on so many.

THE RESPONSE IN THE MARKETPLACE OVER TIME

The last source of information to examine in determining the impact of authentic appreciation in the workplace is marketplace response. Since the publication of the first edition of this book, over 300,000 copies have been sold. Possibly more importantly, from 2013 to 2017 (we don't have any more recent data at the time of publication) the number of books being sold increased every year, where we average selling over 3,000 copies *each month*. (For comparison's sake, the average business book sells 3,000 copies *in its lifetime*.)

Similarly, the rate at which individuals are taking our *Motivating By Appreciation Inventory* continues to increase dramatically. The first 50,000 individuals took the inventory between 2009 and 2014 (56 months), it only took 30 months for the next 50,000, and the third set of 50,000 individuals occurred in 15 months. Currently, over 200 people take it every workday.

Finally, we have over 700 trainers (both internally within organizations and external consultants) who have become Certified Facilitators of our *Appreciation at Work* implementation kit.[51] Our resources are used by multinational corporations, government agencies, hospitals and medical practices, public and private schools, over 750 colleges and universities, nonprofit organizations and ministries, senior care facilities, credit unions and banks, veterinarians, dentists, the US military, and virtually any type of business or organization you can think of.

Clearly, there continues to be a growing desire for authentic appreciation in a wide variety of work settings, and many leaders and organizations are utilizing our resources to help address the need.

WARNING: MISUSING APPRECIATION

Like anything associated with positive outcomes, appreciation can be used inappropriately. When the purpose of appreciation is driven primarily (or in some cases, solely) by financial factors, the game changes. The issue now has moved into the arena of manipulation and displaying certain behaviors for ulterior, selfish motives. Unfortunately, some unscrupulous leaders try to utilize the positive process of communicating appreciation to achieve the organizational benefits without really valuing their employees.

Hence, in the world of employee recognition programs and

strategies to improve employee engagement, a huge "pushback" from employees (and some managers) is occurring. Cynicism and resentment are two common responses from employees who believe employee recognition activities are implemented primarily to increase their productivity and the profits for the company (or bonuses for their managers). When employees feel the underlying motivation for receiving recognition or appreciation[52] is for the benefit of the company or manager, and thus, not being genuinely about them as a person, they react negatively.

Our focus is on helping leaders and colleagues grow in their ability to truly value one another and communicate this effectively. Positive results will eventually occur for the organization if the appreciation is perceived as authentic, but the financial benefits to the organization are not our sole motivation.

THE PURPOSES FOR COMMUNICATING APPRECIATION

What, then, are the core purposes of communicating appreciation for those with whom you work? Ultimately, this is a personal question to be answered by each individual: *Why do I communicate a sense of appreciation to my colleagues?*

Multiple reasons exist for expressing appreciation, but essentially, appreciation for colleagues communicates a sense of respect and value for the person and helps create healthy workplace relationships (which results in the organization functioning better).

Note that appreciation doesn't always have to be for the work they do. Yes, we can appreciate the skills, talents, and abilities a coworker brings to the organization and how they help the company (department, or you) be more effective and successful. But people are more than production units. Employees have

Appreciation doesn't always have to be for the work an employee does.

more value than just what is measured in how much they "get done." (This issue—the relationship between appreciation and performance level—is complex. The topic is explored and discussed more fully in *The Vibrant Workplace: Overcoming the Obstacles to Building a Culture of Appreciation.*)[53]

CONCLUSION

Having an accurate understanding of the concept of appreciation and its role in successful organizations is important for leaders. Some leaders mistakenly believe communicating appreciation is all about "making people feel good." Other managers or leaders attempt to use recognition and appreciation for the sole purpose of achieving secondary financial gains. When they do so, they are playing a risky game of manipulation, which can seriously undermine trust in work relationships.

But when authentic appreciation is communicated, all stakeholders win—the employee, the supervisor, the organization, customers and clients, as well as the family and friends of the employee who get to enjoy a more positive, encouraged individual. The "Return On Investment" from training team members at all levels of the organization on how to effectively show appreciation to one another is highly significant. It improves organizational functioning, decreases the loss of key team members, and creates a more positive workplace environment, providing a holistic Return on Investment for your company.

Making It Personal

1. *If you are a business manager or organizational leader, think of the employees who have left your organization within the last year. It may be wise to talk to people who worked with them, and get a sense of the reason(s) why they left (or to check with the team member who conducted an exit interview with them).*

2. *If you are aware of the reasons why employees have left your company, what have you done to address the concerns they voiced?*

3. *Has your company asked employees to take an employee engagement inventory within the last two years? What results were obtained? In what areas did the employees report positive scores? What areas need improvement?*

4. *Since "feeling appreciated" is one of the major factors in an employee's sense of employee engagement, understand and pay attention to (or investigate) how much your staff feels valued.*[54]

CHAPTER 3

APPRECIATION: FROM BOTH MANAGERS AND PEERS

WHEN WE FIRST STARTED APPLYING the 5 languages to work-based relationships (back in 2009–2010), our initial focus of communicating appreciation within the workplace was on managers and supervisors. Consistent with the belief (at that time) that leadership behavior was one of the most important influencers of workplace culture, we concluded we should try to train supervisors and managers in how to communicate appreciation effectively to their team members.

While this was a good starting point, we quickly learned that to focus *solely* on managers and supervisors was too narrow and was not all that was needed. We began to learn the importance of peer appreciation when one of our training participants commented, "I'm glad that my supervisor is learning how to show appreciation to me. I need and want that. But I also want to know how to encourage Shayla [a colleague] when she's having a rough day."

Most traditional employee recognition programs historically have placed a lot, if not all, of the responsibility for recognizing good work of their team members squarely on the shoulders of managers or supervisors. This is unfortunate and actually creates unwanted negative effects.[1]

Clearly, calling attention to work done well by employees is a good habit for supervisors to practice. When the team feels valued for the contributions they make, a sense of loyalty to and emotional engagement in the mission of the organization develops. But focusing solely on managers and supervisors to support and communicate appreciation to their staff often is an unrealistic expectation that creates problems:

- the manager feels overly burdened with trying to show appreciation to their team;
- members of the team become frustrated with their supervisor when they don't feel they receive enough recognition for the work they do;
- the supervisor can become discouraged with their inability to encourage all team members consistently;
- an overall negativity and disappointment can take hold among the staff in spite of the supervisor's attempts to be positive and encouraging toward their colleagues.

HOW THE WORKPLACE HAS CHANGED

Since we launched our initial research, the workplace culture has been changing dramatically, largely due to the influx of millions of younger employees (late Gen X, millennials, and now Gen Z) into the workforce, as well as the exodus of many boomers from full-time employment into retirement or other forms of work. Younger people's desires and expectations regarding workplace relationships often differ from employees of prior generations.[2]

Younger employees, as a group, tend to desire more collaboration in completing tasks. They want to work together with others to accomplish tasks. This can take the shape of brainstorming initial thoughts to solve a problem, and then delegating different tasks to individual team members. Or some prefer to complete the project together in teams of two and three employees. In either case, the emphasis in many work settings on individual, siloed tasks has declined significantly. (In fact, the term "silo" has come to have a negative connotation for many.)

> As the proportion of employees and leaders from younger generations increases, the supervisor-employee relationship is declining in importance.

Secondly, as the proportion of employees and leaders from younger generations increases, the supervisor-employee relationship is declining in importance. In past decades, there were common sayings such as "people don't leave a job, they leave a supervisor," and this appeared to accurately reflect employees' perspectives at the time.

The influence of a direct supervisor upon an employee's job satisfaction, employee engagement, and employee performance is less impactful now than it used to be (although this still varies significantly across industries and international cultures). As part of an employee engagement survey conducted across a number of companies, employee happiness was found to be much more closely correlated to the connections they shared with their co-workers rather than those they shared with their direct supervisors. In fact, a higher level of happiness was more correlated to connections with coworkers than direct supervisors (by 23%).[3]

THE POWER OF APPRECIATION
FROM COLLEAGUES

Although most employees like to receive positive messages from their supervisor, hearing encouragement and support from their coworkers has become increasingly important. Receiving a compliment or having a colleague report to others how valuable your contribution was to the success of the project is extremely meaningful to more and more employees.

Moreover, colleagues are the individuals who often seem to be most excited to learn how to support their peers. Team members repeatedly tell us statements like: "I really want to learn how to support my colleagues—I want to know how to encourage them when they are having a bad day." While no one has ever communicated that they *don't* want to receive appreciation from their supervisor, many workers seem to understand that their supervisor may not be able to provide all the support that team members need.

In fact, we are finding that the work groups that are most successful in creating a positive work environment are the ones where the manager understands and works to implement the principle of mutual appreciation and encouragement among team members. Not only does the manager accept the responsibility for communicating meaningful appreciation to her or his supervisees, the manager also actively supports their team members in utilizing the *5 Languages of Appreciation* and the results from the *Motivating By Appreciation Inventory* to encourage one another. When this happens, a positive snowball effect begins to emerge, and the individuals within this work group really begin to enjoy working together.

Where does this power created by collegial appreciation come from? In reflecting on this dynamic, the desire colleagues have to show appreciation to one another makes sense on a number of levels:

- Peers know from personal experience the stress and demands their colleagues have to deal with on a daily basis.
- In many settings, there is far more interaction and communication among colleagues than between employees and their supervisors.
- Because of their proximity, coworkers may sense discouragement and the need for appreciation in their peers more quickly than supervisors do.
- While appreciation and encouragement from one's supervisor may be more desired and impactful (for some), support and encouragement from peers may be a more realistic expectation on a day-to-day basis.

THE BENEFITS

Expanding the focus from expecting managers and supervisors to be the sole "appreciators" to include peer appreciation creates numerous positive results for teams:

1. Lightens the load (and perceived load) on managers and supervisors to provide all of the relational support within a team.
2. Supports the focus of younger employees on peer relationships in the workplace.
3. Gets all team members proactively involved (versus wallowing in a "victim" mindset).
4. Builds more relational energy and accountability to keep applying the Appreciation concepts.

5. Allows for appreciation to be applied and communicated even if a manager/supervisor isn't interested or involved.

6. Positively impacts financial results—more so than manager-only recognition.[4]

7. Keeps team members engaged and empowers them to make a difference in their work culture (as opposed to them expecting all appreciation should come from "above").

8. Increases customer satisfaction, according to some research.[5]

We want to emphasize, however, that shifting *full* responsibility from managers to peers is not a good idea. Managers need to lead by example, modeling acts of encouragement to their team, as well as providing the training and resources for coworkers to learn how to effectively communicate genuine appreciation to one another. (Otherwise, the "do-as-I-say-not-as-I-do" approach will lead to increased cynicism and resentment toward the manager.)

IMPLICATIONS FOR ACTION

The implications from the feedback of training participants are important and exciting.

First, this feedback indicates that *individuals at any level within an organization have the opportunity to have a significant impact by showing appreciation and encouragement to those with whom they work.* The task and communication is not solely the domain of those who supervise others. Appreciation from a coworker can be as simple as, "Thanks for getting that report to me quickly, Dan. That's really going to make it easier for me to pull together my presentation without having to rush at the last minute."

Secondly, the conclusion for supervisors is critical: *trying to take on the sole responsibility to communicate appreciation to those whom you supervise will not be as effective as teaching your team members how to encourage one another.* A manager can't carry the load all by themselves, but they can lead and educate their staff in a way that mutual encouragement becomes part of the normal communication pattern among the team.

Finally, *supervisors and managers need to provide the resources necessary for colleagues to learn how to effectively encourage their coworkers* in the ways that are uniquely meaningful to each person. The gap between good intentions and effective implementation may seem small, but in reality the chasm is more like the Grand Canyon. If you are a leader or supervisor, we encourage you to pursue the resources that will help your team effectively apply the concepts of communicating authentic, meaningful appreciation to one another.[6]

CONCLUSION

Just to clarify, we're not proposing that managers give up their efforts to show recognition and communicate appreciation to their team members. Good results follow that plan. But when employees and supervisors consistently (and effectively) communicate appreciation to their colleagues, positive results occur more quickly and are more dramatic in their intensity, and the "staying power" of their effect is longer lasting.

Authentic appreciation communicated from both leaders and coworkers leads to a positive, supportive work environment that others will envy. The result? Positive communication and improved morale to a level we never imagined!

Words of Affirmation

Quality Time

Acts of Service

Tangible Gifts

Physical Touch

CHAPTER 4

APPRECIATION LANGUAGE #1:

WORDS OF AFFIRMATION

JIM RENNARD IS THE TYPE of guy almost everybody likes. He is outgoing, positive, and personable—and, as you can imagine, an extremely successful salesman. With his bulldog perseverance, he has brought in a lot of new business and developed a strong and loyal client base. As a result, Jim has been quite successful financially.

But money isn't what motivates Jim.

Jim loves praise—not inappropriately or excessively so, but what others think of him is clearly important to him. Therefore, if a client says to Jim, "Great job—I really appreciate your help in getting this project done and on time," he smiles and feels affirmed. When his boss says to one of his customers (in front of Jim), "You know, Jim is one of the main reasons for our success. He takes care of his clients, and he makes sure the job is done right," Jim then walks out of the room with a genuine sense of satisfaction. For him, Words of Affirmation is his primary language of appreciation. Certainly, he likes financial success, but if he were not verbally affirmed, he might soon be looking for another company.

Words of Affirmation is the language that uses words to communicate a positive message to another person. When you speak this language, you are verbally affirming a positive characteristic about a person. As with all the languages of appreciation, there are many forms and variations of communicating appreciation through words. Let's look at some of the different ways to express verbal appreciation.

PRAISE FOR ACCOMPLISHMENTS

One way to express Words of Affirmation is to *verbally praise the person for an achievement or accomplishment.* So we tend to praise a colleague when they have done a quality job, or when they meet or exceed our expectations. This was Jim's favorite way to receive appreciation. He thrived on praise.

In the workplace, words are the most common form of appreciation. Since an organization exists to accomplish a mission, when an employee or volunteer makes a significant contribution toward that objective, it seems right to praise them for their work.

Effective verbal praise is specific. The more you can "catch" a staff person doing a task in the way you want *and* call attention to that specific task or behavior, the more likely that behavior is going to occur again. Behavioral research has proven the effectiveness of this principle time and time again. "I like the way you answered the phone in a cheerful tone and offered to help the customer resolve their concern" will probably encourage the receptionist to keep answering the phone cheerfully. Telling a teacher's assistant, "Thanks for showing up early and making sure we were ready to go when the kids arrived," is far more effective than "Thanks, you did a good job today."

It is well documented that global praise does very little to encourage the recipient, and doesn't increase the positive behaviors desired. Many people have reported to us that global comments actually can be demotivating. "I hate it when my boss says, 'Good job, guys!' He could say that to anyone. And to be honest, since my job is so technical, sometimes he wouldn't know if I was doing a good job or not." If praise is to be effective, it must be specific.

AFFIRMATION FOR CHARACTER

Positive character traits in those with whom we work—traits such as self-discipline, perseverance, honesty, integrity, patience, humility, kindness, and unselfishness—are like jewels that should be highly valued. It is likely that most of the people you work with display some of these virtues. The question is, "Have you ever expressed appreciation for these character traits?"

For some of us, it is easy to give words of praise for accomplishments but much more difficult to give words of affirmation that focus on the character of another individual. *Character looks beyond performance and focuses on the inner nature of a person.* Character is the cumulative result of repeated choices over time displayed in a variety of circumstances. Character reveals the behaviors and attitudes that have become part of the person's makeup. It is their default mode of living.

While character traits are not as easily observable as specific accomplishments, they have a far more important long-term impact on an organization. When we fail to focus on verbally affirming positive character traits, we are failing to support and value one of the company's greatest assets: the character of its employees.

Observe your team over time. Note specific instances when they show strength of character. For example, you might say, "Luis, I really appreciate knowing that you are a man of integrity. I can trust you to deal honestly with our finances. That gives me a great sense of security." Or you might say, "Christine, you are a really compassionate person. I have observed the way you respond to people who are expressing frustration. You genuinely seek to understand their perspective. I truly admire you for that." Once you have formulated your own statement of affirmation, read it several times until you feel comfortable in expressing it verbally. Then look for an opportunity to affirm a coworker by focusing on one of their character traits.

For some individuals, commending them for their kindness or honesty or tact means more than any other form of recognition. When their character is affirmed, you "grab their heart" and they respond with loyalty and commitment.

PRAISE FOR PERSONALITY

Another variation of *Words of Appreciation* is *to focus on positive personality traits.* Personality is our normal way of approaching life. There are numerous personality profiles that seek to help people identify both the positive and negative aspects of their own personality.[1] If we understand our own personality patterns, we can learn to "play to our strengths" and minimize our weaknesses.

Here are some of the common—and contrasting—descriptions of different personalities:

- Optimistic
- Aggressive
- Neat

- Pessimistic
- Passive
- Disorganized

- Planner
- Logical
- Talker

- Spontaneous
- Intuitive
- Doer

When a manager or fellow employee observes positive personality traits and verbally affirms them, you help the individual play to his strengths. The very fact that you affirm that personality pattern makes him feel appreciated. The following statements are examples of words of affirmation that focus on positive personality traits:

- "One of the things I admire about you is that you are always optimistic. I sometimes get discouraged, but when I talk with you I always go away with a more positive perspective. I appreciate that."
- "When I walk into your office, I am always inspired. Your desk is always so neat. I wish I were more organized. I really admire that about you."
- "I have observed that while we have a number of people in our department who are big talkers, you're the one who makes things happen. While others are still contemplating what to do, you are actually doing it already. I greatly admire that and appreciate your contribution to the company."

Sometimes calling attention to positive personality traits allows you to communicate appreciation to someone who may be struggling with some parts of their performance. For example, most of us enjoy working with cheerful colleagues more than grumpy ones.

If you can't remember the last time you affirmed one of your colleagues by words of affirmation that focused on their personality, let us encourage you to consciously look for their positive personality traits. Within the next two weeks, verbalize affirmation for a positive trait you observe.

HOW AND WHERE TO AFFIRM

Not only are there many ways to express words of affirmation, but there are also numerous settings in which words of affirmation may be spoken. Understanding the preferred context in which you affirm someone is another part of learning to speak the language of Words of Affirmation fluently. Here are some of the most common settings in which words of affirmation can be spoken effectively:

Personal, one-on-one

A private conversation with one of your staff can be deeply encouraging. A quick word such as, "Steve, I just wanted to let you know I appreciate your hard work and commitment to getting the job done right," can be significant. In fact, the feedback we have received from interviewing individuals is that personal, one-on-one communication is often the most valued and, therefore, the most effective form of Words of Affirmation.

Praise in front of others

Some people value receiving praise in front of people who are important to them. They don't necessarily want a public announcement, but calling attention to the good work they are doing in front of their supervisor, colleagues, or clients really can boost their sense of being valued. Praise given in informal meetings with one's small team of coworkers is a frequent example of public affirmation.

If the purpose of such recognition is to encourage the individual (rather than fulfill a company policy), it is wise to understand what is valued by your team member. Some research has shown that verbal praise given in the context of a smaller group is more valued by workers than awards given in front of large groups.

Written affirmation

Expressing thanks for a job well done through writing is easier and more frequently done in today's world of electronic communication. An email or text message takes just a minute and can be really important to your coworker who stayed late to complete the team's presentation. One manager shared that he consistently texts his team members a note of praise, usually right after the presentation is completed.

Handwritten notes are still valued by a number of workers because they seem more personal and take more time and effort to complete. One nonprofit organizational leader confided to us that he gets numerous positive emails, "which I don't really value that much. But what really means something to me is when someone takes the time to write me a handwritten note." Note, however, that this isn't necessarily true of younger employees (especially twentysomething males), who often report they prefer receiving a quick note electronically.

Public affirmation

Some of us are not shy. We like the spotlight, attention, and hoopla that accompany public recognition for the work we have done. Being recognized in a large group meeting for our leadership in completing a significant task encourages some individuals. Some of those variables are whether the event is planned or a surprise and who is in attendance. Obviously, knowing the type of appreciation preferred by the person being honored is exceedingly important.

But, through polling our training participants over several years, we have found that 40–50% of employees do *not* want to receive recognition in front of a large group. In fact, one woman reported, "I spent the 15 to 20 minutes prior to getting an award from my company throwing up in the restroom."

"THANKS, MISS ROBERTS!"

If ever there were a person who wanted to avoid public recognition of the work she does, Becky Roberts is the poster child. Becky is a quiet, unassuming woman in her late forties who tirelessly works behind the scenes at an inner-city social service agency serving families. In addition to overseeing child care during evening parenting classes and making sure it is staffed with volunteers, Becky also serves single mothers who find themselves in difficult life circumstances. She helps gather baby supplies for them, assists them in getting financial aid, and personally shuttles women and their children to medical and dental appointments throughout the week.

Becky is highly valued and appreciated, not only by the women she serves but also by the professional staff and administration at the agency. She doesn't look for praise from others and would be embarrassed to receive public praise or an award of recognition. But Becky *is* motivated by verbal affirmation—just a different type. She loves to receive notes of thanks from the women she has served, even if they are almost illegible, with poor grammar and spelling. In fact, Becky keeps an "encouragement file" in which she puts notes that she receives. When she is tired or discouraged, she pulls out the file and rereads the notes to help keep her going. She is encouraged even more by the scrawled note along with a hand-drawn picture from seven-year-old Keisha, who wrote: "Thanks, Miss Roberts! I love you! Keisha."

One of the values of having your entire work team complete the *Motivating By Appreciation Inventory* is that you will receive a specific action checklist so you will know not only the kind of affirming words your colleagues like to hear but also the context in which they would most like to receive them. With this information, you can be sure to "hit the mark" (and not create a negative experience) when you seek to give affirming words.

MISSING THE MARK: HOLLOW PRAISE

Words of praise can be encouraging to your workers, but they must be sincere. If they are perceived as being hollow or inauthentic by the recipient, they will not accomplish the purpose of affirmation. Unfortunately, we cannot control others' perceptions of our actions. They may misunderstand our intentions or attribute motives that are not true. However, we should always seek to give affirmation only when we truly mean what we say.

Words of affirmation are most effective when they are given in the context of a positive, healthy relationship. If you are in the midst of miscommunication with your staff member or if there is any unresolved conflict from the past, then deal with those issues first. Your tone of voice and your body language can communicate, "I'm saying these words but I don't really mean it." If you are not able to sincerely express affirmation to your colleague at this time, then silence is preferred until you are able to communicate with integrity and a positive attitude.

THE IMPORTANCE OF WORDS

We have had tens of thousands of employees discover their preferred ways of receiving appreciation by taking the *Motivating By Appreciation Inventory.* At various times, we investigate which languages are most preferred by all employees assessed. Consistently, Words of Affirmation has been the most frequently chosen language of appreciation—approximately 45% of employees. While this is obviously a large majority (and Words of Affirmation is the "best guess" of a colleague's appreciation language if it is not known), the data also indicates that over 50% of employees value appreciation in forms other than words![2]

THE TRAGEDY OF NEGLECT

The greatest tragedy we have observed is that while most managers, supervisors, and colleagues genuinely appreciate the people with whom they work, they often neglect to verbally express that appreciation. I (Gary) had this graphically demonstrated to me. I had spoken at one of the largest publishing houses in the country when a man walked up to me after my presentation and said, "I have worked for this company for twenty years. I think I've done a good job. I have been very creative. My ideas have made a lot of money for the company, but not once in twenty years has anyone ever told me that they appreciated my work." I looked into his eyes as tears rolled down his face. He continued, "How I wish you had given this lecture for our company twenty years ago. I don't expect appreciation every week or even for every project. But wouldn't you think that in twenty years, somebody might express appreciation at least once?" It was obvious to me that his primary language of appreciation was Words of Affirmation, and he had never received them. I walked away from that encounter and wondered how many other employees in organizations across this country would echo his sentiments?

After reading this chapter, we hope that you will make it your goal that none of your coworkers will ever be able to honestly make such a statement. Make it your ambition to look for opportunities to give words of affirmation.

Making It Personal

1. *Have you received a verbal affirmation from a manager or colleague recently? If so, what did they say? How did you feel?*

2. *Can you recall a time within the past few weeks when you verbally affirmed a coworker? If so, what did you say? How did they respond to your affirmation?*

3. *What type of verbal affirmation impacts you the most? What types do you really not prefer?*

4. *Think of someone who, if they did not do their work, would make your daily work life far more difficult. Specify what you value about what they do, and communicate to them how they make your life at work better.*

Words of Affirmation

Quality Time

Acts of Service

Tangible Gifts

Physical Touch

CHAPTER 5

APPRECIATION LANGUAGE #2:

QUALITY TIME

ANNE TAYLOR IS A TEAM PLAYER. She helps organize major events at the private school where she works. Her official position is director of admissions, but everyone knows that Anne is also the lead person for the annual fund-raiser as well as the alumni weekend. She does an excellent job overseeing a large team of volunteers.

Anne enjoys hanging out with her colleagues and supervisor after a job is completed. She said, "I feel like we all need to celebrate together." So, she initiated what has become a tradition: going out for ice-cream sundaes when they have finished cleaning up after an event. It's something that the whole team anticipates. Anne wants her team to feel appreciated and this is her way of expressing appreciation.

After interviewing Anne, we were not surprised to find that her primary language of appreciation is Quality Time. What makes her feel most appreciated is Mr. Johnson, the headmaster of the school, dropping by her office, sitting down in the chair, and saying, "Tell me how things are going." This opportunity to share with him the progress she is making in various projects and for him to hear her frustrations and suggestions is what encourages her the most. Whether Mr. Johnson realizes it or not, these brief expressions of interest in Anne's work makes her feel a part of the team and energizes her to keep going.

Speaking the language of Quality Time to your team is a powerful yet largely misunderstood tool for managers. In the past, many supervisors have interpreted employees' desire for quality time as an inappropriate desire to be their friend, or an effort to "get in good" with the boss in order to have undue influence and receive favors. Our research indicates that this is seldom the attitude of the employee whose primary appreciation language is Quality Time. The employee simply wants to feel that what they are doing is significant and that their supervisor values their contribution. Taking a few minutes to check in and hear how things are going communicates a genuine expression of interest in what they are doing and makes them feel valued.

Even when there is not a question of inappropriate motivation for wanting to spend time, many supervisors react negatively when they learn that one of their team members values Quality Time. "I don't have time to go around and meet with everyone who wants some of my time," Jeff complained. "I already have more to do than I have time for now!"

This reaction points to a couple of misunderstandings leaders often have about people who feel appreciated when they are given Quality Time. As I (Paul) tell leaders in our *Appreciation at Work* training, "Just because one of your team values Quality Time doesn't necessarily mean they want time with *you*. You may be talented and a great leader, but many people enjoy time with their colleagues. That is where they get their support and encouragement."[1]

Secondly, even a little (of the right kind of) time can make a big difference. When going over their team's *Motivating By Appreciation Inventory* results, one CFO shared with her group: "Quality Time is my primary language of appreciation, but I don't need a lot of time. All I really want is for someone to stop by my office occasionally and see how I'm doing. After five minutes, I'm bootin' you because I've got a lot to do!"

> Just because a team member values Quality Time doesn't mean they want time with the boss. Many people enjoy time with theircolleagues.

WHAT IS QUALITY TIME?

By Quality Time, we mean showing the person they are valued by giving them your most precious resource: your time. We are not talking about simply being in physical proximity to another person. Many of us work closely with colleagues all day long, but at the end of the day will honestly say, "I did not have any quality time with any of my colleagues today." How could anyone make that statement? Because a key element of Quality Time is not proximity, but personal attention.

Like Words of Affirmation, the appreciation language of Quality Time also has many dialects. As a matter of fact, the wide variety of types of Quality Time led us to create the specific Action Items section within the *Motivating By Appreciation Inventory*. Why? Because just knowing that a person values Quality Time doesn't tell you the specific kinds of time important to them. As a result, an employee may try to encourage their colleague by spending time with them but "miss the mark" because it wasn't the type of time desired! One reserved administrative assistant told us: "I don't really want individual time with my supervisor. He's fairly intense and I'm pretty shy. He makes me nervous—but I love to hang out after work with a couple of my friends!"

THE "DIALECTS" OF QUALITY TIME

Managers who understand that people have different languages of appreciation will discover that some team members need individual time and attention to feel like they are an important part of the team. It is a wise investment to give them quality time. For those colleagues for whom Quality Time is their primary language of appreciation, a little time can go a long way to help them feel valued, to feel connected with the larger purpose of the organization, and to solidify commitment to getting the project completed.

Jason is the office manager in a multiple-doctor outpatient clinic. He is in charge of the administrative aspects of staffing, billing, and facility-based issues. The group of ten doctors has one leading, managing doctor in addition to several nurses and other support personnel. Jason knows that Dr. Elizabeth Schultz juggles a busy practice, administrative duties, and supervision of interns. Jason greatly valued the time she took each week to meet with him to go over his issues and concerns. Jason reported to us, "I know Dr. Schultz is really busy. But she always makes the time to meet with me almost every week. If she didn't, I know I would feel out of the loop and that my concerns are not really important to her." Clearly Dr. Schultz's investment of time is paying huge dividends by keeping Jason motivated.

Focused attention is one of the most important aspects of Quality Time. Many of us pride ourselves in the ability to multitask. While that may be an admirable trait, it does not communicate genuine interest in the other person when you are spending time with them. Most often, quality time involves giving someone your undivided attention. Don't do other things while you are listening. Resist the urge to answer your phone. Don't text while conversing with a colleague. If you are doing something that you cannot turn away from immediately, tell the individual who wants to talk, "I know you would like to speak with me and I want to give you my full attention. I can't do that right now but if you will give me ten minutes to finish this task, I'll sit down and be able to fully listen to you." Most people respect such a request.

Another form of Quality Time is that of *quality conversation*: dialogue in which two individuals are sharing their thoughts, feelings, and desires in a friendly, uninterrupted context. Quality conversation is quite different from the appreciation language of Words of Affirmation. Affirming words focus on what we are saying, whereas quality conversation focuses more on what we are hearing. Quality conversation means that I am seeking to create a safe environment in which you can share your accomplishments, frustrations, and suggestions. I may ask questions, not in a badgering manner but with a genuine desire to understand your concerns.

Unfortunately, many managers are trained to analyze problems and come up with solutions. This is the "filter" through which they view situations: What is the problem, and what needs to be done to fix it? When problem solving, we often minimize the relationship aspect of the solution. A relationship calls for empathetic listening with a view to understanding what is going on inside the other person. Some managers have little training in listening, so here a few brief practical tips:

1. *Maintain eye contact.* Resist the temptation to look at the ceiling, the floor, out the window, or at the computer screen. Maintaining eye contact keeps your mind from wandering

and communicates to the other person that they have your full attention.

2. *Resist the impulse to interrupt.* The average person listens for only seconds before they interrupt and give their own ideas. If I give you my undivided attention while you are talking, I will be less likely to defend myself or dogmatically repeat my position. My goal is to listen and seek to understand you.

3. *Listen for feelings as well as thoughts.* While you are listening, ask yourself, "What emotion is this person experiencing?" When you think you have the answer, confirm it. You might say, "It seems to me like you are feeling disappointed and hurt because you feel like you were passed over for the promotion. Is that correct?" This gives the individual the chance to clarify feelings. It also communicates that you are listening intently to what they are saying.

4. *Observe body language.* Sometimes body language speaks one message while words speak another. Ask for clarification to make sure you know what they are really thinking and feeling.

5. *Affirm their feelings even if you disagree with their conclusions.* We are emotional creatures. To ignore emotions is to ignore a significant part of our humanity. When a manager says to a colleague, "I can understand how you could feel that way. If I were in your shoes, I would probably feel the same," he is then free to say, "Let me explain how the decision was made." Because you have affirmed their feelings, you are now viewed as supportive, and they are more likely to hear your explanation.

Juliana, an administrative assistant to a sales manager, commented to us, "I know Raphael is busy. He has a lot going and is constantly on the move, but if he would just give me fifteen minutes of focused and uninterrupted time once a week, it would make a big difference to me." Juliana is pleading for quality con-versation. Without it, she does not feel valued.

A third type of Quality Time is *shared experiences.* For some employees, sharing experiences with their colleagues is an im-portant way for them to feel connected and encouraged. Traveling to conferences together, going out to eat, and attending sporting events or other activities in which they have an interest can be an important part of team-building experiences for some coworkers. They may not enjoy a "sit down and talk" conversation, but they feel greatly appreciated when they are invited to participate in an activity with their manager or their colleagues. One self-admitted introverted woman we met said she preferred going to lunch with her colleagues as a group, even if she didn't converse much. She just likes being together with them.

Darin Wooster is a hard worker—just ask anyone who works with him. Whatever he does, he does full throttle. He is willing to work alone, with other team members, or lead a team and delegate to get the job done. When Darin has completed his work, he is ready to "do something" with his colleagues. Nothing pleases him more than for his supervisor, manager, or his coworkers to come along. He loves to go to high-school football games and university basketball games, watch pro football on TV, or go fishing or hunt-ing. When his boss or a colleague invites him to go golfing on the weekend, or come to their home for a barbecue, or take a run together, he feels like he is a valued part of the team.

The desire for shared experiences is the basis for off-site lead-ership retreats or a special team outing like a lake cruise. Our re-search indicates that men whose primary appreciation language is Quality Time often prefer shared experiences as opposed to long sit-down conversations. These men tend to build relationships by doing things together such as golfing, hunting, fishing, going to basketball games, or working together on building a Habitat for Humanity house. To be sure, they talk with one another while doing these activities, but the important thing is that they are *doing* something with their work colleagues.

A fourth subcategory of Quality Time is **working collegially with coworkers on a task.** We have discovered this to be especially meaningful in nonprofit settings and with volunteers. Research indicates that volunteers find their experience more satisfying when two components are involved: they believe that what they are doing makes a difference, and their contributions are recognized and valued by others.[2]

I (Gary) was in Warwick, Rhode Island, two weeks after the area suffered a damaging flood. I had lunch with volunteers who work with the nonprofit organization Samaritan's Purse. They were tearing out carpet and drywall from houses that had been flooded. They were sweaty, dirty, and tired, but they were energized by being part of a team working together to help flood victims.

Younger employees also value working together collegially with their coworkers. Research shows that millennials and even Gen-Xers highly value working collaboratively with others.[3,4,5] Steven, a twentysomething customer service representative, said, "I love being able to work together on projects with colleagues. It's fun. I learn from others and I feel valued when they listen to and consider my ideas as well."

A final variety of quality time is **small group dialogue.** Some people do not feel comfortable talking to their supervisor one-on-one. But in a small group where the supervisor is asking for ideas and suggestions, they feel less intimidated and more likely to share their thoughts. If the supervisor listens attentively and expresses appreciation for their openness, these individuals feel greatly appreciated.

Rick Reed, president of an aerospace manufacturing company,

said, "I have three hundred employees and every three months I lead small group listening sessions in which I ask them to be honest with me about what they think would improve the company. Some of our most significant improvements have come out of these listening sessions. I want my employees to know I value their ideas." This kind of focused attention where the leader is not promoting his own ideas but seeking to hear the ideas of his team members communicates a sense of value to employees. For those whose primary appreciation language is Quality Time, the significance of such focused attention is colossal.

OVERCOMING BARRIERS TO QUALITY TIME

Even in the busy atmosphere of workplaces today, practical opportunities abound to speak the language of Quality Time. In fact, we have learned that it doesn't take a lot of time to encourage others. There are some issues, however, that make it more difficult to communicate appreciation through Quality Time.

Who. As we have worked with organizations, we've received important and consistent feedback from non-manager employees. There is a distinct difference between the Quality Time they desire from their supervisor and what they value from coworkers. One group who worked together reported they like to get together at someone's place, eat, and watch sports together. But it felt awkward to invite their supervisor. To assist in clarifying what employees desire, we expanded the *Motivating By Appreciation Inventory* to allow individuals to indicate *what actions* they desire, and *from whom* they want them.

When. A team of manufacturing supervisors we met with raised another issue: *When* do we speak the language of *Quality Time*? Phil, a manager in his midforties, said, "I have to be honest with you. I love hanging out with my friends. But time is my most valuable resource. I have three kids and my wife, and they come first. Although I'd love to go to a game with my colleagues, my commitment to my family comes first. So if I'm going to spend time with you guys, it's going to have to be connected to the workday." This led to a healthy discussion of ways to spend quality time with coworkers during the context of the workday (including maybe meeting briefly before or after work).

Where. In the corporate world, we often speak of teamwork, but those teams do not always work in close proximity to one another. In fact, more and more team members work remotely these days. While working from different locations presents some challenges in communicating appreciation, we have found it *is* possible to spend Quality Time.[6] For example, setting up a time for a videoconference with a coworker to chat and "catch up" can communicate that you have been thinking about them and want to find out how they are doing.

How. Spending time with others requires a positive attitude, but the following scenario will be familiar to many. The tradition in many offices is for everyone to go to a restaurant for dessert whenever a key team member is promoted or moves to a different department within the organization. Everyone shows up physically, but often it is clear that not everyone is there *emotionally*—people show up late, criticize the restaurant, and generally exude a bad mood. Most everyone else is thinking the same thing—"Why did you bother to come? We don't need a wet blanket on our party."

When you do something resentfully, out of a sense of obligation, the message sent to colleagues is not "you are valued," but rather "I have more important things to do than being here with you." Additionally, communicating a sense of being rushed (by frequently checking the time), or allowing yourself to be interrupted by a phone call, or texting a reply on your cellphone does not demonstrate a sense of value to others. Genuine appreciation always requires sincerity.

CONCLUSION

Showing appreciation by spending time with work associates can take different forms, but the impact on your team members can be significant. When Quality Time is an individual's primary appreciation language, he or she will thrive when they receive time with those they value. However, when they feel ignored or left out, they tend to become discouraged and disgruntled. Quality Time is the best investment you can make in the life of these individuals and will pay huge dividends. Time invested in speaking this language of appreciation may well mean the difference between a motivated employee and one who simply does what is necessary (and who leaves the organization prematurely.)

Making It Personal

---

1. *On a scale of 0–10, how important is it for you to receive quality time with your supervisor? Your coworkers?*

2. *What types of Quality Time do you enjoy? Does what you prefer depend upon whether it is with your supervisor or team members?*

3. *What kinds of Quality Time are realistic in your work setting? Which ones don't really fit your work environment?*

4. *Have you ever experienced a difficult life event and a colleague or supervisor took time just to listen and be empathetic? What impact did that have on you?*

5. *How (and when) is working together coopera- tively on a project demonstrated at your workplace?*

Words of Affirmation

Quality Time

Acts of Service

Tangible Gifts

Physical Touch

CHAPTER 6

APPRECIATION LANGUAGE #3:

ACTS OF SERVICE

MARGARET HARTMAN (AFFECTIONATELY called Maggie by her friends) is a fireball—the kind of worker you want on your team. She has lots of energy, works hard, and is extremely efficient. She is a team leader, able to get her colleagues excited about completing the project.

Maggie doesn't work for praise or recognition. She has a caring attitude, and she intrinsically enjoys working and seeing tasks completed. Therefore, praising her or giving attention to her accomplishments really does not motivate her.

What really encourages Maggie is when others pitch in and help her get things done. She views herself as being "technically challenged" and is especially affirmed when someone helps her with advanced computer work. Maggie, who is only five feet tall, feels greatly encouraged when coworkers help her reach things that are on the top shelf. She loves to hear a teammate say, "Maggie, is there anything I can do to help?"

Maggie's primary language of appreciation is Acts of Service. When others reach out to help, she feels appreciated.

For people like Maggie, demonstrating appreciation through acts of service communicates caring. These individuals have the perspective: "Don't tell me you care; show me." For them, actions speak louder than words. Therefore, giving them a gift or verbal praise can often be met with indifference. They are thinking, "What I could really use is a little help."

While many people in our culture are motivated to get involved in social service projects, the idea of serving someone in their workplace is a foreign concept to them. In prior generations, there was a more individualistic environment within many work settings. People had clearly delineated individualized roles, tasks, and responsibilities. This is still true in many companies, but working together collaboratively, especially among younger team members, has become more highly valued. Although working together in teams to complete tasks has its own unique challenges, collegiality in the workplace—helping one's team members—leads to more successful organizations.

True leadership, whatever your position in the organization, requires a willingness to serve others—both one's customers and one's colleagues. Unfortunately, this perspective does not seem to be well developed among many in the workplace. Some supervisors believe "leading" is telling others what to do, while some employees have a very individualistic perspective: "It's their job; if they can't handle the responsibility, tough."

But here is a common scenario: You have a major project to complete, with the deadline closing in. And, through external circumstances no one could have predicted, you are behind and are working long hours to get the task done. If no one comes alongside to help and ask, "Is there something I can do to help?" and you

True leadership, whatever your position, requires a willingness to serve others.

are left to struggle on your own, this can be extremely discouraging to those who value Acts of Service as an act of support and affirmation. But when a colleague or supervisor assists in getting the task done, it can be extremely encouraging and creates a sense of camaraderie to the staff as a whole.

I (Paul) once worked in an office in which a number of people pulled together to produce a large and complex presentation. To complete the task, it took the combined effort of the financial advisors, graphic designers, technical writers, computer technicians, and administrative assistants. We had a major presentation to complete by the next morning that included PowerPoint slides as well as a large amount of printed material to be delivered in three-ring binders. We were behind schedule, but all of the team members, including the president of the company, stayed late to complete the task. It was a team-building experience. Each individual sacrificed for the benefit of the whole. We had a deep sense of satisfaction when the task was completed. (We also realized that we did not want to repeat the experience, so we retooled our process to make sure it didn't happen again.)

HOW TO SERVE EFFECTIVELY

Providing assistance to one's colleagues is a powerful expression of appreciation, especially to the individual whose primary appreciation language is Acts of Service. Such acts of service will normally be viewed as beneficial. However, several strategies can make the process more effective:

Make sure your own responsibilities are covered before volunteering to help others. Some people are so interested in helping others that they tend to "leave their post" (to use a military concept) and not complete their own work. This is analogous to the high school student who wants to help others get their home-work done but doesn't get his own work completed.

In the work setting, most jobs are interrelated. When one job is left incomplete, the consequences are felt by many. Your other-wise well-intentioned effort to help a coworker may be viewed as shirking your responsibilities. On the other hand, one employee may complete his task before others. When she uses the time as an opportunity to help a coworker, rather than taking a personal break, the assistance will likely be viewed as a sincere act of service.

Ask before you help. It is always critical to ask first when con-sidering helping a colleague. Even when you know an individual's primary language of appreciation is Acts of Service, you need to check with them first to see if they would like assistance on the cur-rent task. If you dive in to help on a task when the coworker does not want help, it can create tension rather than encouragement.

A caveat exists, however. Most individuals, when asked if they could use some help, will almost automatically answer, "No, I'm good. Thanks." Often it is important to offer a second time, being a bit more specific. "Really, I have 20 or 30 minutes over lunch that I have free. Isn't there something I could do to help a little?" In many cases, team members will respond more positively with a suggestion to a follow-up offer.

One worker said, "I usually appreciate the help of a colleague, but in certain situations I would rather do it myself. If someone wants to help me, I would prefer that they simply ask, 'Would you like me to help you with that?' I will be happy to give them an hon-est answer." If you want your acts of service to be received as an expression of appreciation, it's always better to ask before helping.

Don't assume you know what help they want or need. Some-times we assume that we know what would be helpful to others, but misread the situation. One Accounts Payable clerk shared, "My desk was a wreck, with papers and files strewn everywhere; I was feeling overwhelmed. One of my colleagues walked by and saw the frustration on my face and asked if she could help. Of course, I say 'no' initially, but she said, 'Are you sure?' I told her, 'I know it looks like I need help with paperwork but, really, I need to have some phone calls made to a few clients to let them know I will get back to them later this week. If you wouldn't mind making those calls for me, I could spend the time straightening up and organizing my desk.' She did what I asked, I got my head together (and my desk!) and felt a lot better."

If you are going to help, do it their way. Individuals whose personalities tend to be perfectionist resist the help of coworkers because they want the task done a certain way. So when helping out a colleague, it is important to clarify how they want the task done. [Note: this is not the time to show them a "better way" (that is, *your* way) to complete the task.] If you want your efforts to be appreciated, you must be willing to do it in the way that your colleague will feel that the task was "done right." Asking, "How would you like me to do this?" is a great way to start.

This issue is repeatedly reinforced to us by a familiar group of employees—administrative assistants. Whether they work for a school principal, an insurance agent, or the president of a construction company, they react defensively: "If they aren't going to do it the way I want, I would rather they just let me do it myself." But when they hear us state the "do it their way" principle, they relax and often say, "Oh, okay. If that is the case, that would be fine."

Serve voluntarily. For an act of service to be encouraging to a colleague, the action needs to be offered voluntarily. An act of service done under the duress of a supervisor ceases to become an expression of appreciation; it becomes simply an act of duty or obedience. If a supervisor desires someone to help a team member complete a task, the process will more likely be effective if the supervisor makes a request rather than a demand. "Anita, would you mind helping Stephan finish that project? We really need to get it done today; I'm not sure he will be able to do it without some help." Anita is now free to say, "I'd be happy to" or, "I will if you want me to, but I won't be able to finish the report for Midwest Supply, if I do." The supervisor then has an option. She can pressure Anita to help, and thus make it an act of obedience or she can say, "Okay. I appreciate your sharing that with me. Let me see if someone else is available." (Or the supervisor may decide to provide the assistance themselves!)

Check your attitude. There is an ancient proverb that says, "Work done with a cheerful attitude is like rain falling on the desert." We think the opposite is also true. Work done with a negative attitude is like a sandstorm blowing through the desert. Receiving help from someone who is grumpy or who resents having to help is not encouraging. Most people would rather do the work themselves than work around a colleague who has a critical attitude. If you choose to help a coworker, make sure you are able to do the task with a positive, cheerful attitude.

Complete what you start. For those individuals for whom acts of service is important, one way to *not* encourage them is to start a task and then leave it incomplete. If you are going to "help," make sure you get the task done. I (Gary) once had a coworker who volunteered to organize my library. I was thrilled. I thought, "Finally, I will be able to locate a book when I need it." However, my enthusiasm was short-lived when, in the middle of the task, my "good Samaritan" informed me that because of other responsibilities she would not be able to continue the project. To this day, I still have difficulty finding the books I'm looking for.

An alternative approach is often beneficial: before you begin, communicate the limits on your time. You might say, "I have two hours Friday afternoon that I would be willing to devote to help get the boxes in the storage room organized. I'm not sure we will be able to complete the task, but if you would like, I'm willing to invest those two hours in at least getting the process started." If the person you are trying to help accepts your offer, they will likely view it as a genuine act of service.

HOW TO HELP: SUGGESTIONS FROM THE WORKPLACE

How you "help out" a colleague really is situation-specific. It depends on the type of workplace and on the role the individual has in that setting. A nurse in a hospital, an elementary school teacher, or a business office manager would each have their own list of acts of service that would be helpful to them.[1] Even though senior care living facilities have workplace characteristics unique to serving their clientele, the appropriate Act of Service would vary depending whether the employee was a cafeteria worker, a receptionist, in accounting, or a nurse manager.

If you know your colleague's primary language of appreciation is Acts of Service, then discovering the specific service that would be most meaningful to them may be as easy as asking the question, "Is there anything I could do for you that would make your work go better for you this week?" Their answer may surprise you, but you will now have valuable information on how you can most effectively express appreciation to that particular individual. We have found that emphasizing "make your work go better" (rather than "easier") and focusing on the present ("this week") provides more useful responses than a global, open-ended "Do you need help on anything?"

Common suggestions for Acts of Service for those who work in general office settings have included: hold my phone calls so I can focus on completing a report; do some clerical tasks for me (copying, filing) so I can work on a more complex project; or order in some food for me so I can keep working.

Most of us aren't capable of fixing someone's computer, but we can find someone who can!

Interestingly, the most frequent Act of Service that office employees report to us is: *get my computer to work correctly.* When I (Paul) reported this to a large group of managers of a major software firm, they started to boo me (in a teasing manner), to which I bantered back: "No, really! This is what it is like for the rest of us in the 'real world.' If your computer isn't functioning well, completing your work becomes difficult." Most of us aren't capable of fixing someone's computer, but we can find someone who can!

Manufacturing firms and assembly factories present some unique challenges in utilizing Acts of Service as a language of appreciation. In working with floor supervisors of production companies, the issue of helping out workers who are falling behind on the assembly line is a complicated dilemma. On the one hand, supervisors should not "rescue" a worker who is not carrying their weight. On the other hand, there are times when the production process hasn't been fully refined and bottlenecks occur, where certain parts of the assembly process take longer than others. Part of a production supervisor's role is to identify these bottlenecks and reallocate resources (workers, machines, supplies) to the area that is slowing down the overall process. In this setting, providing extra workers to help out is not really an act of service; it is good management.

MISSING THE MARK:
DOING WHAT *YOU* THINK NEEDS TO BE DONE

As we mentioned earlier, the most common way to miss the mark in expressing appreciation by serving others is to do a task that *you* think would be helpful, but really isn't what would be most helpful from your colleague's perspective. When providing an Act of Service, three questions can help you be more likely to do something that is perceived as valuable and supportive:

1. What would be helpful to you?
2. How would you like the task(s) done?
3. When would be the best time to help?

When we demonstrate that we are willing to help our colleagues in the ways most beneficial *to them,* rather than what is convenient for us, we communicate that we value and respect them (and how they do things). Sincere acts of service out of a genuine effort to help others can be deeply meaningful to the recipient and often develop a deep sense of camaraderie.

JOHN LEE: APPRECIATION IN ACTION

John is a low-key kind of guy—not real flashy, the kind of person that you wouldn't pick out in a crowd. But he is "there" consistently. At the nonprofit where he volunteers, John is always one of the first to arrive on Saturday morning to help cook breakfast for the residents of the homeless shelter. If it has snowed, he shows up early to shovel the walk. He typically does the tasks that are demanding physically, take a lot of time, and aren't a lot of fun to most people. He washes the pots and pans after breakfast, vacuums the dining hall, and takes the van to pick up food at the food bank.

John doesn't expect praise. Nor does he enjoy going out to eat or attending special activities with others. He would prefer to work by himself. Trying to keep the conversation going makes him feel uncomfortable.

However, when John's volunteer coordinator shows up on a Saturday morning and works alongside him—cooking, serving up the food, and cleaning the kitchen afterward—John knows that his supervisor values and appreciates the work he does. That is important to him. Clearly, John's primary language of appreciation is Acts of Service.

Demonstrating your appreciation for those you work with by serving them can be a very low-key, yet effective way of encouraging coworkers. If Acts of Service is the primary appreciation language of an individual, then they are energized when colleagues offer to help them. When they feel appreciated, they are deeply motivated to continue using the abilities they have for the benefit of the organization.

Making It Personal

1. *How important to you are acts of service, on a scale of 1 to 10?*

2. *What is an act of service someone could do that would help make your work go more smoothly?*

3. *This coming week, look for colleagues who are working hard to complete a task with an upcoming deadline. Consider asking them, "What could I do that would help you in getting your task (or project) done on time?"*

4. *When someone is helping you on a task, what is important to you about how they help you? What should they do (or not do)?*

Words of Affirmation

Quality Time

Acts of Service

Tangible Gifts

Physical Touch

CHAPTER 7

APPRECIATION LANGUAGE #4:

TANGIBLE GIFTS

RON ENJOYS HIS WORK. He is the plant manager for a family-owned firm that manufactures athletic equipment—helmets for football, baseball, and biking; soccer shin guards; football shoulder pads; and padding of various types for hockey, lacrosse, and other sports. Through the years, Ron has worked his way up through the organization. He gets paid well and generally enjoys his job. He appreciates the "attaboys" and the "high fives" he sometimes receives from his boss when the plant is running smoothly.

But what really makes Ron feel valued is when his boss shares with him some of the company's tickets to sporting events. Two or three times a year he is offered tickets to see some of the local teams play—the Chicago White Sox, some Bulls tickets in the winter, or football tickets to see a game at Northwestern University. He especially appreciates being able to go to the Ohio State game since he grew up in Ohio.

Sharing the tickets is not a big deal to the family owners, but it means a lot to Ron when he can take his son to a game, or go with a couple of buddies. Since the family doesn't share tickets too often with nonfamily members, the fact that they give them to Ron makes him feel genuinely appreciated. Obviously, Ron's primary language of appreciation is Tangible Gifts.

THE CHALLENGE OF TANGIBLE GIFTS

Giving the right gift to a person who appreciates tangible rewards can send a powerful message of thanks, appreciation, and encouragement. Conversely, giving a gift to someone who doesn't really appreciate gifts has little impact; the wrong gift can actually be offensive to the recipient. The challenge of giving the correct gift to the right person is a primary reason why many employers no longer give gifts for Christmas, for work anniversaries, or birthdays. However, to totally eliminate the giving of gifts as an expression of appreciation leaves many employees feeling unappreciated.

Jen, who manages the office at a dental practice, said, "Verbal praise is nice. As for quality time, I don't really care to spend time with most people at work (with the exception of a couple of close friends). And having someone pitch in to try to help me with my work isn't that encouraging to me. I would prefer to do the work myself. However, give me a gift card to go out for a nice meal or tickets to the theater—that is something special to me."

When we introduce the concept of showing appreciation to employees through tangible gifts, some people's eyes light up and they say, "Yes. Show me the money!" But we are not talking about raises or bonuses—that is part of the contract between the organization and employee. Financial compensation is tied directly to job descriptions and reaching agreed-upon performance levels.

In this context, tangible gifts are usually small items that show you are getting to know your coworkers personally and what they enjoy. In fact, a key aspect of a meaningful gift in showing appreciation is that it is *personal*. The issue isn't how much you spent or the monetary value of the gift. The gift should reflect that you are getting to know them and what they enjoy. The statement "It's the thought that counts" is clearly true in this situation. Individuals who value gifts as an act of appreciation tend to react negatively when everyone is given the same item (or sometimes, a generic gift card) because to them it demonstrates the giver didn't think about what each person would enjoy.[1]

GIFTS: THE WHO AND THE WHAT

There are two key components necessary for tangible rewards to be truly encouraging to those who receive them:

First, you need to give gifts primarily to those individuals who appreciate them. While a gift is extremely important to some individuals, it provides very little affirmation to others. Our research with over 100,000 employees found that Tangible Gifts is the least chosen language of appreciation through which individuals want to be shown appreciation. *Only 6% of employees choose Tangible Gifts as their primary language, and 68% report it is their least valued appreciation language.*[2]

Why is this point especially important for Tangible Gifts? Because most employee recognition programs have a heavy emphasis on "rewards." In fact, a major industry has grown up around giving gifts to employees as a way to reward them for longevity or demonstrating desired behaviors, to the tune of more than $1 billion worth of rewards given to employees annually. And yet, that isn't really what makes most employees feel truly valued.

The second key component is: You must give a gift the person values. Two tickets to the ballet are not going to make some guys feel warm and fuzzy. The idea of sitting in the cold on a Sunday afternoon at a professional football game literally will leave many women cold just thinking about it. However, if you can match the concert tickets with an employee who enjoys music, you have expressed appreciation in a way they will long remember. The same is true of the football tickets. If you are a manager, you may be thinking, "This is too difficult. I don't have time to figure out who wants what. Therefore, it is easier not to give gifts at all." We understand the frustration, but just to give up will leave some employees feeling deeply unappreciated.

The critical nature of giving the right gift to the right person is one reason we created the Action Checklist for the *Motivating By Appreciation Inventory.* Even though it is helpful to know that an individual's primary or secondary language of appreciation is Tangible Gifts, the gift giver still has the dilemma of determining which gift to give. But when a supervisor knows what specific gifts would be valued by the individual, they now have the information necessary to show personalized appreciation to their team member. The Action Checklist takes the guesswork out of gift giving. We have found that supervisors and colleagues are more willing to invest time, effort, and money to get a gift when they know it will be meaningful to the recipient.

Food is, of course, a favorite gift in the workplace. Bringing in a colleague's favorite type of coffee, buying bagels or donuts for the team to share, ordering in pizza for Friday lunch—all are common examples of using food to express appreciation to one's colleagues. Astute observers can individualize the shared gift by making sure they buy the types of donuts or pizza (or healthier options) that various team members like. And don't forget quality chocolate!

After food, gift cards are the second most popular workplace gift. But the reality is that many supervisors and colleagues do not have a lot of extra money to personally fund a $25 or $30 gift card for their coworkers.

In one factory setting, we worked with the company's leadership to solve this problem. The management team agreed that they wanted to support their supervisors in encouraging the company's line workers through the use of tangible gifts. So they set aside a special fund (at first just $500 as a trial), and directed the human resources director to work with the supervisors to find out what kind of gift cards or event tickets the employees would like. The HR director then purchased the gifts and had them available for supervisors to utilize with their team members. However, the supervisors were required to send a handwritten note along with the gift, to ensure that it was personalized and gave evidence of time and effort on their part. The supervisors appreciated the practical and financial support from the company, and the employees were openly excited to receive gifts of encouragement that were meaningful to them.

When we talk about tangible gifts as a means of showing appreciation to coworkers, this does not always mean the gift is a "thing." In fact, more often than not, the gifts that people appreciate fall in the category of "experiences" rather than things. These types of gifts include:

- Tickets to sporting events (basketball, baseball, hockey, football)
- Gift cards to restaurants
- Tickets to cultural events (theater, major art exhibits, concerts)
- Small vacations/retreats (a weekend at a bed-and-

breakfast or Airbnb)
- Certificates to a spa or a free round of golf
- Shopping "bucks" at a local mall or online
- Gift cards to a housewares store or for children's clothing

Often team members will chip in on such gifts.

In volunteer settings such as working for a nonprofit organization, serving at one's church, or feeding the homeless, giving monetary gifts to volunteers seems incongruous. It feels awkward (both to the giver and receiver) to give volunteers a card of thanks with a monetary gift enclosed when you are serving a holiday meal to homeless families. But there are ways to give a small item to a volunteer (or a staff member of a nonprofit organization) that are meaningful but don't cost much, if any, money: a coupon to make them a special meal (and bring it to their apartment), volunteering to babysit their kids for an evening, offering to use a talent you have to help them practically (for example, hemming some pants or hanging a shelf).[3]

"TIME OFF" AS A GIFT

One issue we are frequently asked about is: "What about getting some time off as a gift?" In discussing this issue with workers as well as business owners and managers, time off seems to fit best within the category of a benefit they receive. It is a gift (as opposed to Quality Time, which involves being able to spend time with those valued by you).

For a while, "time off" was seen as something that younger employees (millennials and Gen X) primarily wanted. But we have found that "time" has become the most valued resource for most employees, regardless of age group. As a result, being given some time off of work has become highly desired and can take a variety of forms:

- Being able to come in late on a certain day
- Having the freedom to take a longer lunch break (possibly to run some errands)
- The ability to leave work early to go to a grandchild's sporting event
- Taking some "comp time" after completing a big project requiring lots of extra hours

MARIA: NO TIME TO SHOP

Maria loves to shop. However, Maria is frugal. She has two kids in college and holds a responsible position as head of the customer relations department for a financial services firm. Finding time to shop is a challenge for her.

When her supervisor, Jermaine, found out that receiving gifts was important to Maria and that she was a frustrated shopper with no time to shop, he arranged to give her a half day off (with pay) along with a $50 gift card to the shops in the largest mall in the area. You would have thought he was giving a child with a sweet tooth unlimited access to an ice-cream shop and telling her to "eat up!" Maria was elated. She eagerly looked forward to and planned out the shopping trip and talked about her experience for weeks. In her mind, Jermaine was the best manager she had ever worked for. She was strongly motivated to do her best on the job.

That is the power of giving tangible gifts to those who appreciate them. When you find the right type of gift for the person, they feel encouraged and energized to continue to give their best.

MORE THAN A MUG

Those who do not understand the true spirit of showing appreciation through a gift often miss the mark in their attempts to give gifts to others. They fail to understand that it is not solely receiving a gift that matters. Rather, showing appreciation through tangible gifts is effective when the gift shows that the giver has spent time and energy thinking about the gift. They have answered the questions, "What would this person enjoy? What are their interests? What would make them feel special and appreciated?"

Conversely, thoughtless gifts—those gifts bought hastily in response to tradition or a feeling of obligation—with no real personal investment of time or reflection not only miss the mark but also communicate a negative message. The gift seems to be a perfunctory act and not a real expression of appreciation. Such gifts do little to improve relationships. Unfortunately, some leaders and supervisors confuse the "gifts" businesses use as marketing materials (mugs, pens, mouse pads) with items meaningful to their valued employees.

"BAD IDEA": EXAMPLES OF GIFTS
NOT TO REPLICATE

One of the fun aspects of our work is learning from those we are training. Regrettably, we have heard a number of bad examples of gifts given—both at a personal level and organizationally. Here are a few:

- a box of candy for a severe diabetic ("I wondered if they were trying to kill me!")
- logo wear as the *only* gift ever given ("I feel like a walking billboard")

- a photocopied note "We appreciate you!" with a mint taped to it on Employee Appreciation Day (over 1/3 of the nurses in the department resigned within 90 days after this incident)
- leftover marketing trinkets after a convention (with an email to the rest of the company: "To show how much we appreciate all of you, there are leftover items in the break room from our booth at the recent convention. Take whatever you would like!")
- mugs and pens with the company's old logo (left over because the company updated their brand)

And the winner of the worst gift given—last year's calendars![4]

CONCLUSION

When you know that receiving gifts is the primary language of appreciation of a fellow worker, and you choose a gift that you know they would appreciate, you are showing that you are getting to know them and that you took the time and effort to think about what they would enjoy. A small gift, regardless of the cost, can make a huge impact. One participant in our *Appreciation at Work* training shared: "One of my friends attended a conference, and in the exhibition hall he saw an item he knew I would like and brought it back for me. Even though it didn't cost him anything (it was free), I was 'jazzed' because he saw it and thought of me."

Making It Personal

1. On a scale of 0–10, how important to you is receiving gifts?

2. If you said 7 or above, what kind of gifts do you most appreciate?

3. What gifts have you received from coworkers or your supervisor in the past year? Which ones really "hit the mark" for you?

4. What gifts have you seen or experienced (sometimes given organizationally) that missed the target? Why do you think that was the case?

5. What ideas do you have for new or different types of gifts that people in your workplace might enjoy?

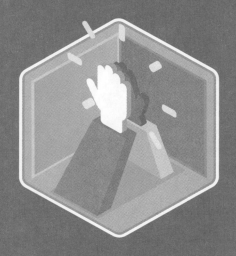

Words of Affirmation

Quality Time

Acts of Service

Tangible Gifts

Physical Touch

CHAPTER 8

APPRECIATION LANGUAGE #5:

PHYSICAL TOUCH

TOUCH IS CONTROVERSIAL.

Physical Touch is the language of appreciation that draws the most comments and intense reactions from individuals when we are giving presentations about the 5 Languages of Appreciation. Comments have included "I can't wait to hear how you are going to deal with this," and "Physical touch in the workplace—are you kidding?" Nonverbal reactions can range from inquisitive smiles or a nervous laugh to an obvious discomfort or audible "hmmph."

If you have taken the *Motivating By Appreciation Inventory*, you probably observed that Appreciation Language #5: Physical Touch is not included. There is a reason for this. When we first started investigating how best to apply the love languages to work-oriented relationships, we included all five of the love languages even though we knew it would be a challenge to translate the language of touch appropriately.

But as we began to work on the assessment tool for the

Appreciation at Work training process, we discovered that there were a limited number of situations involving touch that were appropriate in the workplace. We attempted to create question-naire items that would be sensitive to cultural norms but that were also meaningful in work settings. Some of the questions included:

- "I feel important when someone gives me a firm hand-shake as a means of communicating 'Job well done.'"
- "I feel appreciated when someone gives me a 'high five' when I have done a good job."
- "A simple pat on the back by a supportive friend inspires me to persevere through a difficult task."
- "When a personal tragedy occurs, I appreciate a hug from a close associate."

There are other displays of physical touch that may be accept-able expressions of appreciation—particularly when the team is celebrating an award or the completion of a difficult project. A pat on the back may be entirely appropriate for the team mem-ber who has pulled off a significant sale. However, the appropri-ateness of these actions is highly individualized, and depends on the person, the type of work relationship, and the organizational subculture in which it occurs. Some actions are fine for certain individuals but would make others feel uncomfortable. An office in, say, Atlanta may be more comfortable with appropriate touch than their counterparts in Boston. And some ethnic cultures are much more at ease with physical touch than others. Recognizing these variables, the challenge is to find appropriate expressions of physical touch in work-based relationships.

Physical touch is a normal part of life in most (but not all) rela-tionships. For example, I (Paul) was having lunch with a friend and we were discussing this issue. He stated, "It is a tough one. You can't leave touch out completely. I just left my office and when I found out my assistant had finished a long-term project this morning, I spontaneously put my hand up for a 'high five' to celebrate. She finished the high five, we laughed, and I moved on." On the other hand, one *Appreciation at Work* training participant freely shared with the group: "I don't want *anyone* to touch me, *anywhere, any time.*"

At the same time, we know that physical touch in the workplace can be problematic. As we were testing the *Motivating By Appreciation Inventory* with managers, supervisors, and workers, they repeatedly expressed concern about physical touch in the workplace. Comments from business supervisors included: "I understand the value of the 'touch' language but the touch items make me nervous." "I could see including the 'touch' items in some settings, but I think they could create problems in others."

In our initial research, we found that Physical Touch was rarely anyone's primary language of appreciation in the workplace. And frequently, it was the least important language for most respondents. So, it seemed that when compared to the other four languages of appreciation, physical touch was clearly less important to most individuals in their relationships at work. This data, along with some highly negative reactions by those who had been unfortunate victims of sexual harassment, led us to focus the items of the *MBA Inventory* on only four languages of appreciation.

Interestingly, however, we have heard some negative reaction to Physical Touch not being included in the inventory. One CEO of a large organization had been described to us as an "ex-military hard guy" and the HR director wasn't sure of his support of the concept of communicating appreciation in the workplace. Surprisingly, the first comment he made was, "You know, I disagree with your position on leaving Physical Touch out of the inventory."

He then explained, "Throughout school, I was highly involved in sports and we were always giving high fives, slaps on the back and even hugs when we made a good play. I miss that form of celebrating when good things happen." And there are subcultures for whom physical touch is a normal part of their everyday relationships—both personal and at work. We have had numerous individuals from a Hispanic background state that they wished Physical Touch was still a part of the inventory.

IS THERE A PLACE FOR PHYSICAL TOUCH IN A WORK SETTING?

Many have asked us, "Is there any place for physical touch in the workplace?" This question seems to be most often asked by those who value physical touch in their personal relationships.

We believe there *is* a role for appropriate touch in work-oriented relationships. My (Gary's) academic background is cultural anthropology. In every culture there are appropriate and inappropriate touches between members of the opposite sex, and appropriate and inappropriate touches between members of the same sex.

Appropriate physical touches are a fundamental aspect of human behavior. In the area of child development, numerous research projects have come to the same conclusion: babies who are held, hugged, and touched tenderly develop a healthier emotional life than those who are left for long periods of time without physical contact. The same is true of the elderly. Visit a nursing home and you will find that the residents who receive affirming touches have a more positive spirit and generally do better physically than those who are not touched. Tender, affirming physical touch is a fundamental language of love and appreciation.

What is true for infants and the elderly is also true for adults in the workplace. Affirming, nonsexual touches can be meaningful expressions of appreciation to coworkers. One young single worker said, "It's funny that no one hesitates to touch a baby or pat a strange dog, but here I sit sometimes dying to have someone touch me and no one does. I guess that we don't trust letting people know the fact that we all like to be touched because we are afraid that people will misinterpret it. So we sit back in loneliness and physical isolation." This young woman was not asking for sexual touches. She was acknowledging the emotional need to be touched. Physical touch is a way of acknowledging another person's value and can be deeply encouraging.

ALL TOUCHES ARE NOT CREATED EQUAL

The touches that make *you* feel affirmed may not make *another person* feel affirmed. We must learn from the person whom we are touching what he or she perceives as an affirming touch. If you put your hand on the shoulder of a coworker and their body stiffens, you will know that for them your touch is not communicating appreciation. When someone withdraws from you physically, it often indicates that there is emotional distance between the two of you. In most business interactions, shaking hands is a way of communicating openness and social closeness. When on rare occasions one individual refuses to shake hands with another, it communicates the message that things are not right in their relationship. On the other hand, when you put your hand on a colleague's shoulder while verbalizing affirmation to them, and they respond, "Thanks, I really appreciate that," you will know that both the verbal affirmation and the physical touch have been received in a positive way.

Also, there are implicit and explicit touches. Touches that are implicit are subtle and require only a moment and are often given without a lot of thought. A pat on the back, a quick handshake, or a high five are examples of implicit touches and are common expressions of physical touch in some work settings. Explicit touches normally require more thought and time. An extended handshake while saying to the person, "I really appreciate what you did; I will never forget the effort you poured into this task" may well communicate your appreciation very deeply to the individual who values physical touch.

If you grew up in a "touchy-feely" family and touching comes naturally for you, you will likely carry that trait to work with you. It will be extremely important for you to determine whether the touches you typically give to others are received as affirming touches or if they are irritating to others.

The surest way to find out the appropriateness of physical touch is simply to inquire. You might say, "I grew up in a 'touchy-feely' family. I know that not everyone appreciates that. So if my giving you a high five irritates you, please let me know because I value our relationship."

Almost instinctively in a time of crisis, we reach out to touch one another because physical touch is a powerful communicator of love and concern. In a time of crisis, more than anything we need to feel that others care about us. We can't always change events, but we can survive if we feel loved and appreciated.

> It is critical to remember that the *recipient* is always the authority on what is acceptable touch.

Even in these situations, in the work setting, it is always best to ask if the person would appreciate a hug (either verbally or nonverbally by opening one's arms as an invitation). Rushing up and giving a hug to someone who is either not expecting one or who prefers more personal space may not be experienced as supportive to *them,* even though you may want to show support by giving them a hug. It is critical to remember that the *recipient* is always the authority on what is acceptable touch. Saying "I need to give you a hug!" is not a sufficient reason for violating someone else's boundaries. (Unfortunately, we've seen this happen.)

PHYSICAL TOUCH AND SEXUALITY

The recent attention to sexual harassment has highlighted the danger of touching a member of the opposite sex in a way that is considered sexually inappropriate. This type of touch will not only fail to communicate appreciation; it may result in much more serious problems as well.

Guidelines established by the Equal Employment Opportunity Commission indicate that sexual harassment takes place when one or more of the following conditions exist:

1. An employee submits to sexual advances as a necessary condition of getting or keeping a job, whether explicitly or implicitly.

2. The supervisor makes personnel decisions based on the employee's submissions to or rejection of sexual advances.

3. Sexual conduct becomes unreasonable and interferes with the employee's work performance or creates a work environment that is intimidating, hostile, or offensive.

Unfortunately, such sexual harassment is not rare. More than half of American women have experienced unwanted and inappropriate sexual advances from men: 30% report unwanted sexual advances from male coworkers and 23% have endured them from men who had influence over their work situation.[1] It has become obvious that sexual harassment in the workplace is a huge issue that needs to be combatted on many levels, and we support the efforts to do so.

PHYSICAL TOUCH AND ABUSE

Physical abuse is a sad reality in Western culture. It is important to note that individuals who have been the victims of physical abuse in relationships often are sensitive to any type of physical contact. Although most physical abuse occurs in personal relationships and in the home, regardless of where the abuse has occurred, individuals rightfully develop a greater need for personal protection and a desire for more personal space. Many times, colleagues or supervisors will have no idea that their teammates have experienced physical abuse (either in their past or in current relationships). Thus, we all need to be cautious in the use of appropriate physical touch in our workplace relationships.

BEYOND THE CONCERNS: THE BENEFITS OF PHYSICAL TOUCH IN THE WORKPLACE

Despite the challenges associated with touching in the workplace, we believe the potential benefits of *appropriate* touch are significant enough not to abandon this language of appreciation altogether. Researchers have demonstrated that positive forms of touch do occur in the workplace.[2] Appropriate physical touch in the workplace has been shown to impact supervisor effectiveness in relationships,[3] and increase perceived sincerity when apologizing.[4]

There appear to be two primary purposes of appropriate physical touch in work-based relationships: celebration and support.

Spontaneous celebration among colleagues is the most common reason for an action of "connecting" physically at work. Touch is a means of expressing excitement and joy. A high five for completing a major project, a fistbump for solving a problem, a congratulatory handshake for closing a large sale, or a pat on the back when a colleague receives an award—all are examples of celebrating together through physical touch. Cross-cultural researchers have found that a pat on the back is almost universally accepted as an act that communicates appreciation (which is important to know as more organizations have teams comprised of individuals from different cultures). Interestingly, business schools have begun to research the impact of touch on individuals' behavior in work-based interactions.[5] A sense of camaraderie, mutual respect, and pride in accomplishment are common results when team members share physical expressions of celebration.

Communicating care, concern, and empathy is the second purpose of appropriate touch in relationships at work. We must remember that supervisors, managers, and employees are *people* first and foremost. And each of us has a life outside of work: family, friends, homes, problems. Sometimes what is happening outside of our day-to-day work life is highly significant and impacts our functioning at work. A family member is hurt or hospitalized, you have a serious car accident, a close friend dies, your home is broken into and possessions are stolen—all are examples of life circumstances that will affect us at work. When we are experiencing challenging situations personally, for many people the automatic response is to offer some form of physical support—a hand on their shoulder, a brief hug. When used appropriately, touch also has been shown to positively affect educational learning, emotional healing, and to create a sense of acceptance. Touch can communicate a variety of positive messages in relationships: a sense of trust, connectedness, and caring.

So, while we do not believe communicating encouragement and appreciation through physical touch is foundational in most work-based relationships, neither do we believe the workplace should become a completely "touch-less" environment.

How can you determine which coworkers may view physical touch as an expression of appreciation? Observe the behavior of your colleagues. Do they frequently pat others on the back, give high fives, or hug others? If so, you can explore whether receiving an affirming touch from you would be received as an expression of appreciation. Typically, those individuals who freely touch others in an affirming manner are the same individuals who would welcome affirming touches from others. On the other hand, if you never see a colleague touch others and if, as noted above, their body stiffens when someone touches them, then you will know that physical touch will not be received as appreciation.

> Touch can communicate a sense of trust, connectedness, and caring.

CONCLUSION

You may wish to do a little real-life research yourself. We believe you will find that daily life observations affirm that physical touch is a language often used in the workplace. Watch how others interact when they have a positive collegial relationship. Observe how people respond when something good happens to someone in the workplace. Take time to notice the number of handshakes, fist bumps, high fives, pats on the back, and other physical gestures. Be especially alert in less formal settings such as over a meal, in an after-work social setting, or at a company picnic. You may be surprised at the amount of encouragement that is expressed through physical touch in a warm, supportive, positive fashion.

Making It Personal

1. *What types of physical touch in the workplace do you consider affirming?*

2. *What kinds of touches make you feel uncomfortable?*

3. *Among your colleagues, who are the "touchers"? What guidelines or boundaries do you think would be good to communicate to them regarding what is appropriate physical touch to you?*

4. *Looking back over this past week, what types of physical touches did you give to others? How did they respond?*

5. *Whom have you encountered who seemed to draw back from touching? Do you think it would be good to have a conversation with them clarifying what is / isn't appropriate touch to them?*

CHAPTER 9

DISCOVER YOUR PRIMARY APPRECIATION LANGUAGE:

THE MBA INVENTORY

HOW CAN WE, AS MANAGERS and employees, figure out what our teammates' languages of appreciation are, and the specific actions most meaningful to them? Out of the five fundamental languages, each of us has a primary appreciation language. It is the one that speaks most deeply to us emotionally. Having heard the five appreciation languages—Words of Affirmation, Tangible Gifts, Acts of Service, Quality Time, and Physical Touch—some individuals will immediately recognize their own primary language. Others, because they have never thought of appreciation in this paradigm, will be uncertain of their primary appreciation language. This chapter is designed to describe how the *Motivating By Appreciation (MBA) Inventory* helps you "hit the target" when trying to communicate appreciation to your colleagues.

The *Appreciation at Work* model is based upon the core

principles found in the five love languages:

1. There are different ways to communicate appreciation and encouragement to others.
2. An individual will value a certain language more than another.
3. The most effective communication of appreciation and encouragement occurs when the message is sent in the language of appreciation most valued by the receiver.
4. Messages of appreciation and encouragement in languages not valued by the recipient will tend to miss the mark.

Being able to apply the languages of appreciation to work relationships first requires identifying your own language of appreciation. We developed the *MBA Inventory* to provide an easy, reliable, and valid tool for individuals, employers, and supervisors to accomplish this goal. Over the past ten years, we have field-tested and researched the inventory so that it can provide an accurate assessment of an individual's primary and secondary languages of appreciation.[1] The inventory will also reveal the language that is least meaningful to you.

The *MBA Inventory* is composed of thirty paired statements that compare different ways of communicating encouragement to coworkers. The respondent is asked to choose the statement that more accurately describes the way in which they are encouraged or feel appreciated by those with whom they work. From the pattern of responses chosen, the individual's primary and secondary languages of appreciation are identified.

Along with this book, you were given a registration code that allows you to take the inventory and obtain an individualized report on your responses. The registration code is printed on the inside of the back cover.

To take the *MBA Inventory*, go to mbainventory.com. During the registration process you will be asked to enter your name, email address, some demographic information, and your registration code. Then you will be directed to the *MBA Inventory* items. After choosing your preference for each of the thirty paired statements, you will learn your primary and secondary languages of appreciation, as well as the language that is least meaningful to you.

After completing this portion of the inventory, you will have an opportunity to specify the actions within your primary language of appreciation that others can use if they wish to express appreciation to you in the most meaningful ways.

While it is genuinely helpful to understand your coworkers' language of appreciation, it is far more helpful to be able to identify those unique actions that clearly communicate appreciation to each individual. This eliminates wasting time and energy trying to show appreciation but "missing the mark" on what specific actions are most important to them. For example, two employees may both have Quality Time as their primary language of appreciation but one may prefer individual time with their supervisor, while the other prefers working together with their colleagues.

WHAT JUANITA WANTS MOST

Juanita is a dedicated staff member of a nonprofit organization that works with inner-city youth. She works tirelessly matching adult mentors with teen protégés. She screens potential mentors, provides training for them, and interviews young people and their parents who are looking for positive role models. She then facilitates the development of what will hopefully be long-term mentoring relationships. Juanita doesn't make a lot of money, but what motivates her to continue her work is people verbally acknowledging the value of the work she is doing. She feels appreciated when she receives:

- A word of thanks from a customer she has helped to solve a problem.
- A smile and a gentle "thanks" from her colleagues whom she helped learn a new task on the computer.
- A word of commendation from her supervisor such as, "Juanita, I am really appreciative of your dependability; being here every day on time, and even a little bit early."

But don't take Juanita up in front of a group and praise her publicly. And *definitely* don't give her an award for her exemplary service at the annual fund-raising event. Both of these would embarrass her.

How would Juanita's boss know this? Most probably, only as a result of a negative reaction by Juanita in response to an action she did not want to have happen. (Obviously, it would be far better to know her preferences ahead of time.)

ACTION CHECKLISTS

As we created the *MBA Inventory,* we received feedback on the best ways coworkers could apply the information they received about others' preferred languages. So we added a section that asks respondents about the specific actions they desire within their primary language of appreciation. For example, if they value Acts of Service, what would be most helpful to them? We also learned that a desired action depends on the work relationship, so the inventory asks *from whom* they want various actions ("supervisor," "colleague," "direct report," or "anyone").

That is the purpose of Action Checklists—to give managers and supervisors specific actions that are most meaningful to each member of their team. Therefore, after your primary language is identified from the *MBA Inventory*, you will be asked to choose specific expressions of that language that are most meaningful to you.

Upon completing the Action Checklist, a fully individualized report will be generated that identifies your primary language of appreciation, your secondary language of appreciation, the language that is of least importance, and a list of the specific ways others can best encourage you based on your primary language of appreciation. You can then save your report, print it, and email it to your supervisor or colleagues at work. Additionally, group result reports can be created to obtain the *MBA Inventory* results for everyone in a large group.[2]

Imagine the difference it could make if each of your colleagues learns how to express appreciation and encouragement in the primary language of their coworkers! We can assure you that the emotional climate, the level of work satisfaction, and the general morale of the group will be enhanced.

WHAT IF MY COWORKERS HAVE NOT TAKEN THE *MBA INVENTORY*?

We recognize that many employees will be reading this book as individuals. Their manager, supervisor, and colleagues may be unaware of the book or the inventory. If you wish to be a positive catalyst for improving the climate of your work environment, our first suggestion is that you give a copy of the book to your manager or supervisor.[3] Encourage them to read it and share with you their impressions.

We believe that many managers will see the value of the *MBA Inventory* and also will want to explore the resources available to apply the results with their team members.[4] If your supervisor is not that interested, then you may wish to share the book with your closest coworkers, suggesting that if they would each take the inventory, you could discuss the results together and begin to practice effectively communicating appreciation with one another.

We have found a lack of interest from higher-level managers to be one of the most frequent obstacles for applying appreciation in the workplace and have addressed this issue thoroughly elsewhere.[5]

Be encouraged, however. Many times we have seen an individual spark the interest of other employees, and the word about appreciation spreads informally—to the point that whole departments and divisions have learned to communicate authentic appreciation to one another. There is little to be lost and much to be gained in trying to lead your coworkers into being more effective communicators of appreciation.

DISCOVERING YOUR COWORKERS' LANGUAGE

If your coworkers have not taken the *MBA Inventory* but you would like to more effectively express appreciation to them, here are some practical suggestions to try to discover their primary appreciation language.

First, a caveat. Directly asking a colleague how they want to be shown appreciation will not yield much helpful information. This topic is somewhat awkward in our culture and most people will just respond: "I don't know, tell me 'thanks,' I guess." Trying to observe what they do to show appreciation to others also is difficult because there aren't many data points to observe. How often do you observe someone communicating appreciation to a colleague?

> Many people who enjoy giving gifts are not that impacted by receiving gifts themselves.

Additionally, our research has indicated that about 25% of the population typically speaks one appreciation language but wishes to receive another language. This is especially true for Tangible Gifts. Many people who enjoy giving gifts are not that impacted by receiving gifts themselves.

Here are three informal ways of trying to discover the primary appreciation language of your colleagues:

1. *Observe what they request of others.* If you often hear coworkers asking for help with projects, then Acts of Service may be their appreciation language. The coworker who says, "When you go to the conference, would you pick up some freebies for me?" is requesting gifts. If colleagues are regularly asking friends to go shopping with them, take a trip together, or come over to their house for dinner, they are asking for quality time. If you hear them ask coworkers, "Does this look all right? Did I do the report the way you wanted? Do you think I did the right thing?" they are asking for words of affirmation. Our requests tend to indicate our primary appreciation language.

2. *Listen to their complaints.* The things about which an individual complains may well reveal their appreciation language. Brad was about six months into his first job after college when I (Gary) asked him, "How are things going?" "Okay, I guess. However, it seems like nobody really appreciates what I do and that what I do is never enough." Knowing that he was familiar with the languages of appreciation, I said, "Your primary appreciation language is Words of

Affirmation, right?" He nodded his head while he said, "Yes. And I guess that's why I'm not all that happy with my job." Brad's complaint clearly revealed his primary language of appreciation.

If a coworker complains that their colleagues no longer have time for them, their language of appreciation is likely Quality Time. If they complain that no one remembers their birthday, even with a card, their language is likely Tangible Gifts. If their complaint is that no one ever helps them with tasks, then Acts of Service is likely their appreciation language. Related to this, we have found that an individual's preferred language of appreciation is often the language in which they are most easily offended. Essentially, they are sensitive to *both* positive and negative messages sent through this channel.[6]

3. Explore how they are encouraged. While most of us do not think a lot about how we feel appreciated, culturally and emotionally we connect more with feeling "encouraged" or "discouraged." Therefore, you may gain some clues about a person's preferred language of appreciation by asking them, "When you are discouraged, what is something that encourages you?" Or, "When you've been discouraged in the past, what has someone done that you have found to be encouraging?" There often is limited utility to this process, however, because the range of actions or responses will tend to be fairly small, whereas having individuals go through the *Motivating By Appreciation Inventory* broadens their exposure to many additional ways that they may feel appreciated and encouraged.

APPRECIATION IS SITUATION-SPECIFIC

Workplaces and roles within each workplace differ significantly. As a result, we have developed customized inventories for various settings to make them as accurate and practical as possible.

Currently, we have specific versions of the *MBA Inventory* created for government agencies, schools, the military, medical settings, non-profits and ministries, remote employees, and general work settings.

The primary differences among the versions are in the action items. For example, Acts of Service may differ significantly depending on whether the coworker is an elementary school teacher, a nurse in a hospital, works for an inner-city social service agency, or is deployed with the military overseas.[7] Please note: the code provided with this book is for a general work setting but can be "upgraded" for other specific inventory versions.

Making It Personal

1. *After you take the* MBA Inventory *for yourself, think about and share the results with other colleagues regarding what you learned about yourself.*

2. *If you are a manager or supervisor, consider providing a copy of this book to those who work under your supervision so they can take the inventory. Alternatively, groups of codes can be purchased for those who would not be interested in reading the book.*

3. *A wide range of resources has been developed to assist managers, HR professionals, corporate trainers, and employees in applying the concepts of the 5 Languages of Appreciation—including resources for small groups, online "train-the-*

trainer" courses, an individual online tutorial, as well as free resources for posting other results of your group. Please go to appreciationatwork. com/train to see the valuable resources.

THE DIFFERENCE BETWEEN RECOGNITION AND APPRECIATION

YOUR WORKPLACE PROBABLY has some kind of "recognition" program. Employee recognition programs have become a standard part of most businesses—it is estimated that 85–90% of all organizations in the US now have some form of employee recognition activities.[1] Recognizing employees for a job well done or when they reach a chronological milestone (such as having worked for the company for ten years) are the most common reasons employees are recognized. And, in most cases, a sincere attempt is being made by leadership to express appreciation to their employees through these programs. Interestingly, however, one study found that, across a wide range of companies, only 53% of employees knew that their organization had a recognition program.[2]

At first glance, employee recognition may appear to be the

focus of this book. To draw that conclusion would be a mistake. We strongly believe that, while there may be some overlap, a distinct difference exists between recognition and appreciation. While we support public recognition of quality work and recognize the importance of performance-based rewards, we believe the focus on recognition and rewards is too narrow and has significant limitations.

EMPLOYEE RECOGNITION ISN'T WORKING

The truth is, the vast majority of employee recognition programs aren't working, as many HR professionals have acknowledged to us. In fact, when we ask employees and managers about their employee recognition program, some of the most common responses we receive are apathy ("Yeah, we have one but I don't go to the award ceremonies"), sarcasm ("Big deal. A certificate, a gift card, and some applause every five years"), and cynicism ("The administration doesn't give a rip about us. They are just going through the motions to look good to the Board").

Why the negative reactions? Here are a few reasons. First, *there is a disconnect between celebrating length of service and motivation.* The most common reason (85%) for employee recognition is length of service.[3] We believe it is important to recognize and honor those who have served the organization for a long time. However, recognizing someone for being employed for five years does not provide them a lot of motivation to do their job well. Additionally, our culture clearly has changed. Longevity and loyalty to an employer are no longer highly valued by most employees.

Longevity and loyalty to an employer are no longer highly valued by most employees.

Secondly, the *rewards given often aren't*

that meaningful. Employers report that the most frequent rewards given for high levels of accomplishment are certificates and
plaques (80% of the time), followed by gift cards.[4] Additionally,
many times when recognition is given, no explanation is given
why the employee is receiving the award. In fact, one of our *Appreciation at Work* participants reported: "I received the 'Employee
of the Month' award, and I have no idea why."

Also, *we know that many people do not like public recognition and
attention.* Every organization that we have taken through our *Appreciation at Work* training has been asked, "Which of you would
really rather not be recognized in front of a large group?" Typically,
30–40% of the group raises their hands. (For some groups, the
percentage is even higher—administrative assistants: 60–70%,
librarians: 90%.) The intensity of reactions is also notable. We
have heard such comments as, "You can give me the award, but
you'll have to drag me up front to receive it!" Managers and
supervisors need to understand and accept that *just because* you
would like the public recognition does not *mean that all of your team
members will.*

Finally, the languages of appreciation model is a more effective approach to encouraging colleagues than the narrower recognition and award approach, which has a number of limitations.
Among them:

Limitation #1: Emphasis on performance

While recognition focuses primarily on *performance* or the
achievement of certain goals, appreciation focuses on the *value of
the individual employee.*[5] The level of performance of the employee
is certainly a consideration—but not the only consideration.
There are times when high-performing employees do not do well
on tasks or make a major mistake. Do they cease to be valuable

to the organization during this time period? Also, not all employ-ees are high achievers, but all employees need appreciation and encouragement. While recognition focuses on what the person does, appreciation focuses on who the person is.

This point was raised by a team leader during one of our training sessions. Donna asked, "Should appreciation only be expressed when team members are performing well? Isn't there a place for appreciation even when someone messes up? Other-wise, it seems appreciation becomes totally performance-based." We completely agree with this perspective. Although supervisors want to support and reinforce positive behaviors demonstrated by their staff, workers need to be encouraged when they are having an "off day" too. In fact, we could argue that when a colleague re-acts inappropriately to a situation or when they have made a mis-take, this creates an opportunity for a supervisor to demonstrate appreciation for the employee *in spite of* their performance in this one circumstance. A comment like, "Matt, it looks like you're hav-ing a challenging day. Is there anything I can do to help?" may mean a great deal to your team member—and communicate that your support of them goes beyond their daily performance.

Managers also need to keep the context of the behavior in mind. An employee may be going through a period of extraor-dinary trauma in their personal life: experiencing the illness or death of a loved one, having relational struggles at home, or deal-ing with challenges with their own physical health. All these can detract from an individual's performance at work.

Managers and supervisors who utilize encouragement and appreciation can address these factors in a positive, supportive manner, in a way that programs of recognition do not. Particularly during these difficult times, managers need to be actively com-municating appreciation, encouragement, and support for their team members—not based on performance or achievement but grounded in the value you hold for them as a person.

It is true that rewards do tend to motivate those who receive them to continue their high level of performance. However, they are less effective in motivating those who do not receive the reward. On the other hand, appreciation, when expressed in the primary appreciation language of the individual, tends to motivate each team member to reach his or her potential. When we feel appreciated, we are motivated to "climb higher." Conversely, without appreciation, we often settle into mediocre performance or, worse, discouragement.

Yvette, an administrative assistant to the CEO of a financial services company, reported to us, "My greatest goal is to help Eric [the CEO] be as successful as he can be—because when he is successful, then the whole company benefits. When he is pleased with my work and lets me know that he appreciates what I do for him, it just motivates me all the more—I get a surge of energy and I'm ready to tackle any problem."

Limitation #2: Missing half the team

The rewards most often offered in programs of employee recognition typically include only two of the languages of appreciation: Words of Affirmation and Tangible Gifts. In these presentations, someone makes a speech extolling what the employee has accomplished or their contributions to the company over the years. Then they are presented with a gift of some sort. If the primary appreciation language of the recipient is Words of Affirmation or Tangible Gifts, they will likely feel appreciated. However, our research shows that only about half of employees prefer appreciation to be shown through these two languages.

Over 165,000 employees have taken the *Motivating By*

Appreciation Inventory,[6] which identifies an individual's primary language of appreciation, secondary language of appreciation, and their least valued appreciation language. We have analyzed the data from their responses and found the following themes.

Employees overwhelmingly choose receiving Words of Affirmation as the primary way they like to be shown appreciation in the workplace. Although almost half of all employees (over 45%) prefer receiving verbal praise as their primary language of appreciation,[7] this demonstrates that *over half* of all employees prefer appreciation communicated in ways other than words.

Secondly, even though employee recognition programs heavily emphasize rewards (especially in incentive-based programs), only 6% of employees choose tangible rewards as their primary language of appreciation. As we have seen, for many employees, Tangible Gifts is their least favored way to be shown appreciation. So, by just utilizing verbal praise along with a gift, recognition programs "miss the mark" in communicating appreciation in the ways preferred by approximately half of their employees.

Some recognition proponents dismiss these concerns by saying, "They must like it because they smile for the photos." Or, leaders who themselves like public recognition (for example, high-performing financial advisors) have a hard time believing that someone wouldn't want to be praised in public. This line of thinking leads to a key concept we emphasize in the training we provide: *to be an effective leader, you have to learn how to lead those who are different from you.*[8] We believe it is important to listen to workers' reactions and comments, and respond appropriately.

Finally, it is a generally accepted premise that only the top

Often the same top performers are recognized repeatedly over time, while the middle 50% of team members hear nothing.

10–15% of employees are recognized for outstanding performance. And often the same top performers are recognized repeatedly over time (which can spark negative reactions from their peers), while the middle 50% of team members hear *nothing*. This solid middle group of employees, who show up "day in and day out," do their work, and contribute to the success of the organization (even though they aren't the stars of the team) are the individuals who are at risk for becoming discouraged and leaving. Remember, 79% of employees who quit their jobs voluntarily cite not feeling appreciated as a key factor for deciding to leave.[9]

Limitation #3: Not perceived as genuine

Too often employee recognition is implemented in an impersonal, top-down corporate policy approach. Not only that, but little or no effort is given to identifying the specific type of recognition the employee being honored would appreciate. Two of the most common complaints we hear regarding recognition programs is that they are *generic* and *impersonal*. The ceremony is the same every year. Everyone being recognized receives a plaque or framed certificate, sometimes along with a cash award. The award is presented by an executive who does not even know the employee. (One person reported, "They wouldn't be able to pick me out of a group!")

Employees know that the recognition program is generated by upper-level management, rather than being personal and individualized. Even more problematic is the skepticism this approach can create as to the genuineness of the appreciation communicated. We believe a critical mistake well-meaning organizational leaders make is approaching employee recognition or appreciation in terms of a managerial directive: "This is something we all are going to do." An automatic undermining of perceived authenticity is the result. Employees frequently ask themselves: "Is my manager doing or saying this because she means it, or because she is supposed to follow the company's recognition program?"

We get significant pushback from team members about this issue. Randy, a staff member at a nonprofit youth organization, said, "I don't want my supervisor to spend time with me just because she's supposed to, since time is my primary language of motivation. If she doesn't want to spend time with me, that's okay. But I don't want her to fake it. That's worse." A perception of insincere appreciation is deadly to an organization, undermining trust in communication at multiple levels.

Thus, when implementing programs of recognition, organizational leaders would be more effective if they allowed team members to freely choose whether or not they would like to participate. We have found that starting with a pilot group comprising individuals who are interested in learning how to communicate appreciation is a highly successful approach. Many who are initially reluctant become interested in the process after they have observed the personal, genuine approach utilized.

Limitation #4: Significant financial cost

Lastly, an additional downside to the recognition-and-reward approach is the cost involved. Many organizations, especially nonprofit organizations, schools, ministries, and social service agencies, do not have the funds available to pay for the gifts that typically come with the recognition/reward approach. And many times, the practice of giving substantial financial rewards for goals achieved is not a "good fit" within the overall context of the mission and values of the organization.

Also, since Tangible Gifts is the appreciation language least valued by employees (by their own admission),[10] it appears that organizations are wasting thousands of dollars in giving gifts to their employees—gifts that have little impact on the staff's morale or sense of job satisfaction.

On the other hand, the *Appreciation at Work* concepts can be put to work in any financial climate, with any size organization, governmental agency, school system, business enterprise, or nonprofit and social service organization. The approach we have outlined does not have to wait for top-level executives to approve and begin facilitating it. The program can be launched at any organizational level by managers, supervisors, or even a single employee who has a desire to create a more positive climate in the work setting.

Dave modeled this fact. He was a mid-level supervisor within his organization. He managed a team of five, but he also belonged to a team of supervisors who reported to higher-level managers, including the president of his firm. Dave knew of the work we were doing on this project and asked if he could have his team take the inventory. After doing so, we met with Dave and his team and went over the results. As we worked over time to implement the appreciation model within their relationships, he shared what he was doing with his fellow supervisors, and they became interested. Over a series of weeks, they continued to listen to Dave's stories about the project and the positive impact it was having on his relationships with his teammates. After a while, the president approached Dave and said, "I think it would be good for the leadership team to go through this process—how do we make that happen?" And so it went.

CONCLUSION

We have seen the consistent application of individualized appreciation and encouragement within a work environment transform attitudes, relationships, and even workplace cultures. We believe that putting into practice the principles we have shared in this book can strengthen the emotional climate of any work setting.

Making It Personal

1. What do you know about your organization's program of recognition? For what are employees recognized? How are they recognized?

2. Have you ever experienced recognition from your organization for length of service? Or for some achievement? How did you feel upon receiving it?

3. How would you describe what you see as the difference between recognition and appreciation?

4. If you had a choice between receiving recognition and appreciation, which would you choose? Why?

5. Do you believe it is possible for an individual (or small group) to begin to make a difference at their workplace by beginning to communicate authentic appreciation to others? Why or why not?

CHAPTER 11

YOUR POTENTIAL BLIND SPOT: YOUR LEAST VALUED LANGUAGE

BY NATURE, WE ALL TEND to speak our own language of appreciation. If Acts of Service make me feel appreciated, then I will pitch in and help my colleagues and be willing to go the extra mile in completing a task. If Quality Time makes me feel valued, then I will often seek out my coworkers to check in and see how they are doing. If Words of Affirmation encourage me, then you can expect that I will give compliments and praise to those with whom I work. If I appreciate Tangible Gifts, then I will likely give gifts to others. If a high five energizes me and makes me feel appreciated, I will likely express my appreciation to others with Physical Touch.

Conversely, if I only do what comes naturally to me, the language of appreciation that I value least will seldom be used with others. If receiving gifts means little to me in terms of feeling appreciated, then I am likely to ignore this language of appreciation. It becomes for me a blind spot. I assume that since it has little value to me, it will be of little value to others. Thus, the coworkers for whom receiving gifts is their primary language of appreciation will feel unappreciated even though in my mind, I am freely expressing appreciation in one of the other languages. Here is an example:

"STACY SUNSHINE"

Stacy Grant is a department manager for a computer graphics design firm. She oversees the Web designers who create websites for their corporate customers. Stacy is an accomplished designer herself and, at the same time, an excellent manager. She enjoys coordinating the team of Web designers in overseeing the production process.

Stacy is a positive, supportive manager who is well-liked. She has a talented team and they work together well. Stacy's primary language of appreciation is Words of Affirmation. She loves compliments on her work, and although she may not admit it publicly, Stacy likes recognition to be given in front of her team members and supervisor. She never gets tired of hearing what a good job she is doing.

Consequently, Stacy attempts to encourage her team members in the same manner. She is extremely generous with praise, frequently telling her team what great work they do, and extolling their artistic abilities. This is good—especially for those on her team who respond to verbal encouragement. Her communication style creates an overall positive atmosphere.

However, Stacy's least valued language of appreciation is Acts of Service. She doesn't want others to help her get her work done.

She would prefer to do it herself. In fact, she views others' offers to assist her as intrusive and more trouble than they're worth. The upshot is that Stacy rarely if ever volunteers to help others when they could use some assistance. This creates tension in her department among those for whom Acts of Service is their primary language of appreciation.

Carolyn, one of the designers in Stacy's department, is a solid team member. Her primary language of appreciation is Acts of Service. She really appreciates it when others step up and help her get a project done when she is pressed for time. Thus, she feels very unsupported when others don't offer to help. When she is feeling stressed about getting a project done, and Stacy comes in and tries to encourage her verbally, the result is not positive:

"Hey, this looks great, Carrie," Stacy says as she comes over to Carolyn's area and looks at the work she is doing.

"Thanks," Carolyn responds. "But I have a lot to get done by 9 a.m. tomorrow before the client presentation. It's going to be a late night." She looks at her boss.

"Oh, I'm sure you'll get it done," says Stacy. "You always do. I appreciate your commitment and follow-through to do whatever it takes to get the job done." She pats Carolyn on the shoulder as she goes back to her office.

"Thanks a lot," Carolyn mutters to herself. "A little help would be appreciated. But no, Miss Stacy Sunshine has to run off, go around and tell everyone what good work they are doing. I'd rather see a little action and hear less chatter."

Stacy thinks she is doing an effective job of encouraging and supporting Carolyn by giving her verbal encouragement.

However, Carolyn is feeling unsupported by Stacy and even resentful of her "lack of consideration." This classic mismatch of two coworkers' languages of appreciation leads to miscommunication and relational tension. In fact, research has shown that 51% of managers believe they are doing a good job of recognizing employees for work well done. But only 17% of their employees agree.[1]

If the issue of Carolyn's feeling unsupported ever came up in conversation, Stacy would probably feel confused and blindsided. "What? How can you feel like I don't appreciate the work you do? Carolyn, I am always giving you lots of compliments about your work. And I even took the initiative to praise you publicly in one of our team meetings in front of the management! I don't understand."

Carolyn might respond, "Stacy, I know you frequently tell me I do good work. But I have to say, sometimes when I'm struggling to meet a deadline, I wish I got some help. Words are great, but some practical assistance would mean more."

And so it goes. Stacy is putting forth initiative to express appreciation, but not in the way that is encouraging to Carolyn. Carolyn starts to feels unsupported and becomes resentful. Stacy then feels like she is wasting her breath trying to encourage Carolyn and becomes discouraged in her ability to manage her team effectively.

THE BLACK HOLE

In astronomy, a black hole is an entity that sucks in virtually every-thing surrounding it—light, matter, energy. Whatever goes in never comes out. A black hole takes and takes, without giving back.

A person's least valued language of appreciation can be experienced as a black hole in the work setting. When a colleague's least important language of appreciation is Words of Affirmation, no matter how much praise you give them, it won't seem to impact them. They will not feel encouraged or appreciated from compliments, notes of appreciation, or recognition in front of team members. You are essentially wasting your energy. The same can be true of any of the languages—spending quality time with team members, doing tasks to help them out, a congratulatory pat on the shoulder, giving them a gift card to a nice restaurant.

> A person's lowest language of appreciation *really* is not important to them. This does not mean that the other person is weird. They are simply different from you.

Let us save you a lot of time and emotional energy, if you are will-ing to accept our input: a person's lowest language of appreciation *really* is not important to them. This does not mean that the other person is weird. They are simply different—different from you.[2]

Understanding and accepting your team members' differences in how they feel appreciated and encouraged is critical to your success as a manager. If you don't fully grasp and implement this reality in how you relate to your colleagues, you may begin to resent those team members who have different languages of appreciation. You may start to feel that they are ungrateful, negative, and don't appre-ciate all that you are trying to do for them. You may conclude that there is nothing that will satisfy them or make them feel like you appreciate their work. This, of course, is not true; thus, knowing that your least valued language of appreciation is likely your potential blind spot in relating to others is an important step in becoming an effective communicator of appreciation.

OVERCOMING THE CHALLENGE
OF YOUR BLIND SPOT

The first step in getting past your blind spot as a manager or colleague is to become aware of it. Assuming you have taken the *Motivating By Appreciation (MBA) Inventory* and identified your least favorite language of appreciation, you now have that information. However, it is likely that you really don't *understand* this language of appreciation.

For me (Paul), Tangible Gifts is my least valued language of appreciation. Certainly, I appreciate receiving a gift card to go out to eat, but it is really not a big deal to me. I can take it or leave it. So it is harder for me to put myself in one of my colleagues' shoes and really understand how they could highly value tangible rewards. I often find myself thinking thoughts like, "They certainly get excited about something that is no big deal," or "I just don't get it. I would much rather get some praise than some money to eat out."

Therefore, I have taken the initiative to talk to some of my colleagues whose primary language of appreciation is receiving tangible gifts. I asked one of my team members, "What about getting tickets to the ballgame is important to you? Why does that mean so much to you?" His response helped me to see the situation from his point of view.

"Because," Joe replied, "first, it shows me that my team leader has taken time and interest to find out something about me personally and what I like. I played baseball in college and still love going to games. Second, he took the initiative and effort to go and get the tickets for me. It shows me that doing what it takes to encourage or reward me is worth it to him."

Once you have identified your least valued language of appreciation, we would encourage you to talk with colleagues for whom this is their primary language of appreciation. Ask them how those actions communicate appreciation to them and how they are encouraged by them. Try to gain a deeper sense of understanding of how others are impacted by your least valued appreciation language. Learning to speak that language effectively with your teammates will then become easier for you.

Leadership studies have shown that successful managers seek to understand the other person's point of view—supervisors, customers, colleagues, and those they manage.[3] If a leader is unable to see another person's perspective, she will be more likely to make wrong assumptions that lead to poor decisions based on inaccurate information.

Thus, if an employee's *MBA Inventory* results indicate that Quality Time is important to them, the wise manager and colleague will take this information seriously. You may not fully understand why spending individual time with them is that important, but you choose to do so because you take seriously what they say. If you wait until you totally get why it is important to them, you may lose a lot of time and opportunities to communicate appreciation— and you may lose a team member in the process.

PLAN TO SPEAK THEIR LANGUAGE

Communicating in our least important language takes effort; it doesn't come naturally. We must think about it more intentionally and try to look for opportunities to communicate appreciation to others in the ways important to them.

To be successful may require planning how you will show appreciation to team members who have a language that you do not value highly. For example, when Quality Time is a supervisor's least important language, that supervisor is not likely to spontaneously spend time with their colleagues. It never enters their mind that this would be something important to do. So a team member who values Quality Time can seemingly "starve" while waiting for this type of appreciation from their supervisor.

A wise manager will take the initiative to schedule regular times with such team members. Essentially, the manager says to herself, "I know that Quality Time is Carmen's primary language of appreciation. I also realize it is not that important to me. So, I'd better put it on my calendar to stop by and see her at least every other week to check in and see how she's doing." What we schedule, we normally do.

Understanding that the language that we value least can become our blind spot in effectively communicating appreciation to our colleagues is highly significant. Taking steps to correct the process can be critical in making sure that all team members feel valued by their supervisor and coworkers.

Making It Personal

1. *What is your least valued language of appreciation?*

2. *Do you have team members or coworkers whose MBA Inventory results indicate that your least valued language is their most valued language of appreciation?*

3. *Can you recall the last time you spoke that particular language to that coworker? Would you be willing to take a moment to make specific plans to speak the primary appreciation language of that employee within the next week? If so, put it on your calendar.*

4. *When you speak their primary language, carefully observe your colleagues' responses. We think it will become obvious that your efforts to express appreciation have been effective.*

CHAPTER 12

APPRECIATION WITH REMOTE EMPLOYEES AND VIRTUAL TEAMS

EMILY IS A YOUNG PROFESSIONAL who started working in customer service while applying to go to grad school. She enjoyed the work, was good at it, and was valued by her employer. When she was accepted into a graduate program in another city, Emily and her supervisor worked out an arrangement where she could continue to perform a number of her duties remotely. The arrangement worked well for Emily—the position allowed for flexible hours (which changed from semester to semester), she was able to earn a higher wage than she would in most part-time jobs, and she could work from home. Conversely, her employer benefited by keeping a valued employee. They were able to use Emily's experience and acquired knowledge to help clients. As a plus, they did not have to train a new employee in the tasks

Emily was doing. Emily was a responsible team member and de-lightful to work with. Her supervisor, Steve, reported: "Keeping her connected with the rest of the team has been a learning pro-cess for us, but we seem to be doing okay: involving her in team meetings virtually, calling and chatting with her occasionally about how her studies are going, and she stops by some holidays when she comes home to visit her family."

More and more American employees are working remotely (and this is true for many other work cultures, as well.) Accord-ing to a Gallup poll in 2015, 37% of US workers say they have telecommuted, up slightly from 30% last decade but four times greater than the 9% found in 1995.[1] In 2016, 43% of American workers reported that they spend at least part of their week work-ing remotely, and the proportion of remote workers continues to increase every year.[2]

A more recent survey of 500 managers and executives found that:

- 53% of companies in the US continue to have standard workplaces, with nearly every employee coming into the office 4 or more days each week.
- 37% have a main office with some people working remotely.
- 10% have no office space at all.[3]

Additionally, employees are spending *more time* working from a distance. According to a Gallup survey, the number of workers who work one day or less from home shrank from 34% to 25% between 2012 and 2016. In the same time period, the number of people working remotely four or five days a week rose from 24% to 31%.[4]

Between 80 and 90% of the US workforce report they would like to work remotely at least part-time, and it has been estimated that 50% of the US workforce have job responsibilities that are compatible with working off-site at least occasionally.[5]

A robust 68% of millennial job seekers said an option to work remotely would greatly increase their interest in specific employers, according to a survey of college students and recent grads.[10] (See the next chapter for more information about millennials.) *These statistics point to more and more work relationships existing in the context of remote locations.* Increasing numbers of employees work in locations separate from their colleagues and supervisor, with "virtual teams" occurring across cities, states, and countries.

The combination of the facts that all employees desire to be appreciated for their work and that more and more employees will be working remotely creates a challenge that needs to be addressed: *How do you effectively communicate appreciation to your team members in the context of long-distance work relationships?*

BENEFITS OF REMOTE EMPLOYEES

Utilizing remote employees can provide a number of benefits: an organization needs less office space, is able to employ specialized team members who are difficult to find locally, and can retain longer-term employees who want to start to transition out of traditional full-time positions.[6] Also, some research has indicated that remote employees are more efficient in their use of time.[7] (It should be noted, however, that there are so many different types of jobs and work conditions within the large group of "remote employees" that this issue will need to be investigated further.)

In the past, employees who spent the *least* amount of time off-site said they felt most engaged. But in the past few years, this trend has changed. Some research has found that remote workers are often *more* engaged with their colleagues than in-office workers are. By 2016, employees who spent 60–80% of their time away from the office had the highest rates of engagement.[8] A key factor was found to make a significant difference—the use of videoconferencing.[9]

APPRECIATION ACROSS LONG DISTANCES

The vast influx of long-distance work relationships into organizations is a major influence in changing workplace cultures. For leaders (and colleagues) who are used to working on-site with team members, long-distance relationships create new dynamics. Specifically, communicating appreciation to remote staff and virtual teams is challenging—but the data from our research shows it can be done.

When working with companies and organizations who have offices across the country and team members spread over the world, one of the first issues raised by their leaders was: "How do we effectively show appreciation to those who work in different states and countries?" Obviously, some common acts of appreciation in face-to-face relationships are impossible—such as refilling someone's cup of coffee when you are going to the break room or stopping by their office to chat.

In response, we created the Long Distance version of the *Motivating By Appreciation Inventory*, which includes specific actions in each language of appreciation that are relevant to long-distance work relationships. (See the section below on "Practical Steps" for examples.) This version of the inventory has been well received and is growing in its use.[11]

But we wanted to make sure that we were meeting the need expressed, so we polled employees and managers who either work remotely or manage others who are in a different location, and found the following results:[12]

- Almost all (98%) of the respondents said "yes," *it is possible to effectively communicate appreciation to colleagues who work remotely.*

- Additionally, *70% indicated that they personally have received a message of appreciation* from a colleague or supervisor within a remote working relationship.

- *81% reported that they have communicated appreciation to a coworker* who works in a remote location.

- Interestingly (to us, at least), there was very little difference in the rankings of how easy or difficult it is to communicate appreciation to remote colleagues in the various appreciation languages. We did anticipate that Physical Touch would be ranked as the most difficult, with Words of Affirmation being the easiest to communicate over a long distance. Our data confirmed our belief.

- Finally, we asked the participants to share *examples of receiving or communicating appreciation to remote colleagues* and also to give *suggestions for communicating appreciation over distance more effectively*. What was interesting to note is that, while there were a few unique twists, largely the two lists were the same. The implication? Many supervisors and managers are currently acting in the desired way.

Do remote and on-site employees desire different forms of appreciation?

Over time, we began to wonder if those individuals who were in long-distance work relationships desired to be shown appreciation in the same ways as employees who worked on-site. That is, do employees who work remotely choose different preferred languages of appreciation than those in the general workforce? To find out, we compared almost 90,000 individuals who had taken the *MBA Inventory* between 2014 and 2018; more than 86,000 had completed the general workplace version and 2,600+ used the Long Distance version.

We found that employees working in long-distance work relationships chose Quality Time more frequently (35%) than workers on-site (25%). The majority of these switched from Words of Affirmation being their primary appreciation language (48% in general work settings to 38% for long distance employees).[13] So it is important to keep in mind that many remote employees value Quality Time with their colleagues more highly than those who work in face-to-face settings. Using videoconferencing to "check in" and including them in team meetings virtually can help these team members feel valued.

THE SINGLE MOST IMPORTANT LESSON

The **single most important lesson** we have learned for effectively communicating appreciation to remote colleagues is that *you* *must be more proactive* than in face-to-face relationships.

One of the biggest barriers to overcome in showing appreciation over a distance is *the lack of opportunity for those brief chance
encounters* that occur when you work in the same location—coming into the office in the morning, while getting something in the
break room, walking through the hallway in the office, or sitting
together in the conference room waiting for a meeting to start. All
of these provide the occasion to be able to chat for a few minutes,
"check in" and see how others are doing. In long-distance work
relationships, these events don't occur.

The result is that most, if not all, interactions with your long distance coworkers are focused on work and the tasks at hand. This, in
turn, can make your relationship feel very cool and distant with no
personal warmth involved at all. One of the best ways to overcome
this challenge is to intentionally schedule some interaction times
focused primarily on "chatting," hearing about what they did over
the weekend, and sharing what is going on in your life as well.

PRACTICAL STEPS

Words of Affirmation

Obviously, technology-based solutions help us communicate
across long distances. Telephone calls, email, texting, and video-
conferences are all accessible methods for communicating appreciation via words. The challenge most supervisors and colleagues
must still overcome is finding the time to do so.

Communicating appreciation verbally is the most common
(and, sometimes, only) method utilized in the workplace—
either orally through a personal thanks or word of praise, or some
written form of communication, like an email, text, or handwrit-

ten note. So the default mode for most managers is to use words with their remote staff.

When we asked employees who work in long-distance work settings for their favorite ways to receive appreciation through Words of Affirmation, they suggested:

- Use multiple formats for communicating—email, texts, talking on the phone, and videoconferencing.
- Send physical (snail mail) notes and cards occasionally. Don't use only electronic media.
- Arrange for the remote worker to join a team meeting virtually and allow time for colleagues to chat and "catch up" personally (like you would do during an informal lunch meeting).
- Be sure and give praise for the team member's work in ways that others are included (copy them on emails, or give a compliment during a conference call).

The problem: Not everyone values words. In our work with tens of thousands of employees, we have found that only about 45% report that their preferred way of receiving appreciation is through words. (Obviously, that means that members of the remaining 55% don't find words of affirmation the most meaningful way of receiving messages of appreciation.)

While communicating appreciation through words is a positive action, doing so primarily (or exclusively) means you are "missing the mark" in effectively communicating with the majority of your team members. Why? Because some individuals view words as "cheap" or have the view that "actions speak louder than words." With these employees, you are wasting at least some of your time and energy by using words alone.

Reaching those employees who value other acts of appreciation can have other challenges, but we have found they *can* be done successfully—but to do so takes more planning and intentionality than in same-location relationships.

Quality Time

For those who feel valued when others ***choose to spend time*** with them, the following actions can be helpful in long-distance work relationships:

- Schedule a call occasionally just to chat and see how work-related tasks are going.
- Give them your undivided attention when you are talking on the phone (don't multitask).
- Set aside some time to talk about non-work related topics at the beginning of a scheduled call.
- Set up a videoconference with your team, as a group, to chat and get caught up with one another personally.

Acts of Service

In the area of providing some ***act of service***, we have found the following actions to be effective in communicating appreciation between long-distance coworkers:

- Agree to schedule a meeting or call when it is convenient for *them*, not according to *your* time zone.
- Assign some staff assistance in completing some menial task for them, so they focus their energy on tasks only they can complete.
- Work out a plan to answer their phone calls or emails for a specified period of time, so they can focus solely on getting a project done.

Tangible Gifts

When **getting some small gift** for your long-distance colleagues, a little extra effort can be quite impactful:

- Find out their favorite lunch spot and arrange to pay for their meal.
- Do some investigation about their preferred place for coffee and dessert and get them a gift card there.
- Send them some food, spices, magazines, or sports memorabilia that are hard to find where they live.

Physical Touch

Actual physical touch in long-distance work relationships obviously is difficult, if not impossible. There are two exceptions, however. First, when team members *are* in the same location for a meeting or conference, an appropriate warm greeting should be the goal. Like appropriate physical touch in the workplace (in general), there are cultural and personal norms that need to be honored. But almost universally, a warm handshake is acceptable. (Conversely, hugs or "kisses" on the cheeks are not welcomed by many.) Warmth can be communicated by a smile, eye contact, and a friendly greeting.

Secondly, experienced remote workers have told us that they often give "virtual high fives" during a video conference (high-fiving the camera), or they send an electronic icon of a fist bump when a task has been successfully completed.

None of the actions in the various appreciation languages, by themselves, are magic. But a little appreciation can go a long way to encourage a colleague, especially when it is in the language of appreciation they value.

MORE APPRECIATION IDEAS
SUGGESTED BY REMOTE EMPLOYEES:

- Scheduling meetings with my supervisor— her spending time to talk to me was important.

- Having "coffee" via Skype to catch up on life outside of work.

- Sending various gifts, a box of candy, flowers, Starbucks cards, T-shirts.

- Emailing funny pictures inspired by recent conversations.

- Managing emails or phone calls once a day instead of multiple times a day to respect my time.

- Allowing a coworker to call and "vent" and share their frustration.

- Making sure the remote worker is brought up-to-date on other issues going on in the office.

- Sending a physical card for a birthday, "sorry for your loss," or other occasion and having people in the office sign it.

- Utilizing videoconferencing (Skype, Go-To-Meeting, Zoom).

- Making sure that issues discussed in the main office are shared with remote employees.

- Checking in to see how their day is going.

- Making travel arrangements for the remote employee to join an annual company celebration.

Additional challenge: Appreciation within *virtual teams*

At *Appreciation at Work,* more and more of our clients are asking for ways to train their employees and supervisors in effectively communicating appreciation across long distances with remote employees (and most recently, demonstrating appreciation among virtual teams where *all* of the team members work in different locations).

Communicating appreciation to remote workers is challenging but doable. But completely virtual teams are another matter. Why? Because often the individuals have never met and their interactions are solely around task completion. As a result, the working relationship the team members have is quite limited in scope.

Attempting to solve the challenge of communicating appreciation within virtual teams has led us to three important observations:

1. Relationships are built upon relating to (and with) one another. True, there are different levels of relationships (acquaintances, friends, close friends, committed long-term relationships). But if your interaction with another person is focused solely on completing tasks, then we would argue that you have a *functional* relationship, not a *personal* relationship. You and your coworkers each bring skills, knowledge, and experience to complete a task or solve a problem. But your interaction may have very little, if any, personal substance to it. This, we think, is a major challenge facing virtual teams (and unfortunately, some teams who work together in the same location!)—they essentially reduce employees to producers and problem solvers (rather than understanding coworkers as persons).

2. To truly appreciate someone, a relationship must exist. You can admire or respect someone from a distance, but to appreciate them, you need to have a relationship with them as a person—not just a resource to help get the project done. We can appreciate something a colleague has done for us (which is a good start), but to value *who they are* requires some personal interaction or knowledge. Their life has some impact on you—their determination and the perseverance they exhibit, how they manage a problem, or how they treat others with respect even when they disagree with them.

3. Appreciation flows from valuing another person. People have often asked, "What if I don't appreciate one of my colleagues? How do I develop a sense of appreciation for them?"[14] Like most feeling responses, you can't just make yourself appreciate them (or alternatively quit being frustrated with them). Feelings are responses that come from how our experience matches our expectations. We have found that the best way to "grow" a sense of appreciation for someone is to get to know them better as a person—where they come from, their background, their current life circumstances. Usually, we then learn something about them that strikes a chord within us, where we better understand them, we appreciate the challenges they are facing, and ultimately, develop more reasonable expectations for them.

Guiding principles for communicating appreciation virtually

These observations lead to two guiding principles for communicating appreciation between virtual team members. First, *for authentic appreciation to be communicated, you must have a relationship with the person.* The longer or deeper the relationship with your colleague is, the more appropriate the appreciation will appear. But unless other steps are taken, attempting to communicate appreciation to

> We have found that the best way to "grow" a sense of appreciation for someone is to get to know them better as a person.

someone with whom you have no (or virtually no) relationship will almost certainly create problems:

a) Your actions and intent will probably be misperceived as manipulative.

b) The interaction will have an awkward quality to it.

c) You almost certainly will "miss the mark" of what makes them feel appreciated.

At best, you will waste your time and energy. At worst, you could damage your relationship to the point they will not want to interact with you at all in the future. The implication? If you are on a virtual team, start to get to know your team members. Spend some time texting, emailing, or "chatting" with them, sharing something about yourself and getting to know them better.[15]

Secondly, *the more specific, the more impactful the appreciation will be.* To be effective, your appreciation should communicate specifically how they have been helpful to you. And, if possible, include some aspect that makes the note or comment connected to them at a personal level (related to an interest they have or something going on in their life). If you cannot think of anything specific they have done that has impacted you, then wait until you have an example. In the meantime, get to know them better at a personal level.

CONCLUSION

While communicating appreciation in long-distance work relationships takes time and forethought, it *can* be done and it is important to do so. Without ongoing appreciation and support for the work they are doing, employees who work remotely are at risk for becoming discouraged, not producing to their capabilities, and eventually quitting.

Take the time and effort to communicate how much you value your staff who work in a different physical location, and the return on your investment will be well worth the cost.

CHAPTER 13

GENERATIONAL DIFFERENCES AND OTHER FAQS

Q1: ARE THERE DIFFERENCES IN HOW VARIOUS GENERATIONS LIKE TO BE SHOWN APPRECIATION?

This is one of the most frequent questions we are asked, with a popular variation being: *Do millennials (or Gen Z) like different types of appreciation than older employees do?*

With the influx of millions of employees from Generations Y (millennials) and Z (born in 2000 or later and just now entering the workforce), understanding the differences across generations in the workplace has become a huge focus. Since we as individuals are shaped by our life experiences, people who have similar life experiences tend to think and respond to situations more similarly than others who didn't share those experiences.[1] Groups of people can share similar characteristics (same age, from the same region, same gender), but there are obviously individual differences within or across group members.

Therefore, *it is dangerous to make assumptions about individuals solely from the group tendencies.* For example, in discussing this topic with a large group of multigenerational workers, one young woman stated, "I'm tired of everyone assuming that I'm a slacker because I'm only twenty-three. It is offensive to me." And in this case it was true—she was identified as a hardworking, young, and rising star. Additionally, the characteristics identified can be true of other groups (for example, not every fifty-year-old employee is a hard worker).

We are not full-fledged experts on the differences that create conflicts between generations. But we have done research on workplace relationship issues related to challenges in communicating effectively across generations.

WHAT OUR RESEARCH SHOWED

We analyzed the responses by over 55,000 employees who took our *Motivating By Appreciation Inventory* between 2014 and 2018.[2] Ninety-two percent were between twenty-one and fifty-nine years old. Interestingly, we had a very even distribution of age groups who took the assessment: 21% were in their twenties, 30% in their thirties, 25% in their forties, and 18% in their fifties.

We compared the responses of the individuals from the different age groups to see if there might be differences in the frequency that they chose their primary, secondary, and least valued languages of appreciation.

With regards to their Primary Language of Appreciation, we found that younger employees desire Quality Time more and Acts of Service less from their colleagues than older employees do. Their rates of desiring Words of Affirmation and Tangible Gifts were essentially equivalent. (There were no practical differences identified with regards to secondary and least valued languages of appreciation.)

PRIMARY LANGUAGE OF APPRECIATION*

	Words	Time	Service	Gifts
Younger Employees (< 29 years old)	46%	31%	17%	7%
Older Employees (30 years old and older)	47%	25%	23%	5%

These results are consistent with a key theme identified with millennials (and potentially Gen Z)—that they highly value collegial relationships in the workplace. [Physical Touch is not assessed by the inventory given the low frequency it occurs within the general population.]

WHAT YOUNGER EMPLOYEES PREFER

We have also observed the following patterns in the *specific acts* of appreciation that younger employees prefer:

Time off.

As is well known, many younger workers desire a flexible schedule and receiving time off (in some work settings, known as "comp time") as a reward for working hard to complete a project. Since in many ways time has become the most valuable resource we have (everyone feels like they don't have enough), it makes sense that free time is highly valued.

Handwritten notes—or not.

For those of us from an older generation, we were raised to believe that one of the highest forms of showing appreciation was to send a handwritten thank-you note. (Remember when you received a nice birthday present from your grandparents and your mother forced you to sit down and write a note?) Times have changed. For many younger workers, the value of handwritten notes has declined. This seems to be especially true for twenty-something males—receiving a handwritten note of encouragement adds *no value* to them (but this is true for only about 50% of twentysomething women).

Rather, what *is* important to younger colleagues is the speed with which they receive feedback. Immediate is great. Today is good. Tomorrow is acceptable. After that, you've moved into the realm of history. So if you want to be effective in communicating that you valued their work on a task, let them know as soon as you can.

Working collaboratively.

When thinking about specific actions within the language of Quality Time, younger team members are more interested in working together with colleagues on a project than older generations are. Baby boomers and older Gen-Xers are fine with working in teams to get tasks done, but they have more of a divide-and-conquer approach where they meet together to determine the common goal and then delegate tasks to accomplish individually. Younger employees generally enjoy the process of hanging out together to work cooperatively to achieve the final product.

Recognizing team accomplishments vs. individual achievements. Related to the preference to work together on projects is the desire to receive recognition and appreciation *as a team,* rather than one or two team members being selected to receive individual accolades (this is similar to many Asian cultures in perspective). In fact, picking out one person as the leader of the effort can actually be offensive—both to the team and to the one receiving the attention.

Q2: WHAT ARE THE FREQUENCIES OF EACH APPRECIATION LANGUAGE ACROSS THE GENERAL WORKFORCE?

As we have noted, *not everyone wants to be shown appreciation in the same ways.* Some people like verbal praise, but others feel valued when you spend time with them. A number of employees feel supported by receiving some help when they are overwhelmed, while others are encouraged if you bring in their favorite cup of coffee or a snack.

While each person gets their own unique report of how they like to be shown appreciation, and these results are often shared across team members, it is also interesting to know "how do my results compare with most people in the workforce? Do most people prefer Acts of Service (like I do) or am I an 'odd duck'?"

As a result, we determined a process to find out how frequently individuals choose each of the appreciation languages as their preferred (and least valued) way of receiving encouragement. When we reached 100,000 employees who had taken the *Motivating By Appreciation Inventory,* the data from their responses was analyzed. The inventory identifies each person's primary language of appreciation, secondary language of appreciation, and their least valued appreciation language.

You can find the full results of our survey in an academic journal,[3] but here is a summary of our findings.

Words of Affirmation are most desired

Employees overwhelmingly choose receiving Words of Affirmation as the primary way they like to be shown appreciation in the workplace. Almost half of all employees (over 45%) prefer receiving verbal praise as their primary language of appreciation.

Why do Words of Affirmation seems to be so desired by employees? First, the high use of words seem to be partially related to enculturation—words have been the way encouragement has been communicated in the workplace historically. Thus, it appears using words is partially a learned behavior. Secondly, showing appreciation through words typically is fairly easy to do and takes less effort than some of the other appreciation languages; thus, using verbal language is easy to use and also to teach to others.

Tangible Gifts are the least desired

Again, the evidence is clear. When asked to compare the various *Languages of Appreciation* in importance to them, *employees overwhelmingly* don't choose *tangible rewards as the primary way they want to be shown appreciation*. In fact, less than 10% of employees identify tangible gifts as their primary language of appreciation. To look at the issue from the opposite perspective, employees choose tangible gifts as their *least* valued way to be shown appreciation almost 70% of the time.

But interpreting the data correctly is important. Employees *aren't* saying they don't want tangible rewards (gift cards, going out to eat, earning a trip) for doing good work—and they clearly won't refuse receiving a gift! But what the data shows is that when choosing *between* Words of Affirmation, Quality Time, or an Act of Service—receiving a gift is far less meaningful than appreciation

"If I receive some gift but never hear any praise, the gift feels really superficial."

communicated through these actions. For example, often employees comment, "If I receive some gift but I never hear any praise, no one stops to see how I'm doing, or I never get any help—the gift feels really superficial."

This is clearly a ***loud and important message for leaders, managers, and HR professionals to hear***—if you are trying to use rewards to communicate appreciation to your employees, you are not only missing the mark, you (and your company) are probably wasting a lot of money!

Quality Time is an important secondary language

While Acts of Service and Quality Time are frequently chosen at a similar rate by employees as their primary language (between 20–25% of the time), some additional data sheds further light on these two appreciation languages.

First, when looking at what language individuals choose as their secondary appreciation language, Quality Time is preferred over Acts of Service. Additionally, Quality Time is the least valued language for about 7% of the population, but Acts of Service is more frequently chosen as the least valued way to be shown appreciation at over twice that rate. Thus, overall, Quality Time appears to be people's second-most-desired way to be shown appreciation.

Finally, it should be noted that there is a slight gender difference, with men preferring Acts of Service slightly more, while women chose Quality Time more frequently. Even though the difference is slight, it is notable.

CONCLUSION

Knowing trends across the workforce can be helpful in understanding your employees' desires for how to be shown appreciation for the work they do. But practically speaking, **the *most* important information is to know how your *individual* team members desire to be appreciated**—and then actively communicate appreciation in the language and actions most important to *them*.

Secondly, **quit thinking that receiving rewards is highly meaningful to employees—tangible gifts *aren't* the primary way over 90% of employees want to be shown appreciation.** Rather, they would prefer some individual time and attention, help on tasks (especially on time-sensitive projects), and to hear specifically what you appreciate about them. Listen up! 100,000-plus employees are talking to you.

Q3: HOW DO YOU COMMUNICATE APPRECIATION EFFECTIVELY WHEN YOU MANAGE LARGE GROUPS OF EMPLOYEES?

When I (Paul) am conducting an *Appreciation at Work* training session with a work group, a common comment and question is similar to what Jack, a manager at a senior-care living center, asked: "I get the concept of communicating appreciation to my team and the need to make it personal and individualized. But I have team members who report to me that I rarely see. They work a different shift or on the weekends and, while we communicate through email, texts, and occasional calls, I really don't have much actual interaction with them. How do I communicate appreciation to them?"

Similarly, Nancy, a nursing manager at a hospital, said: "I oversee 50–70 nurses at our facility. I don't see how I can make this work with that many direct reports." I agreed. Trying to authentically communicate appreciation to that many team members (and in the ways that are important to each of them) is not possible. (I also thought to myself, but didn't say: "Wow, having that many people reporting to one supervisor isn't going to work.")

So, what do you do when you have a large group of employees you supervise? There is no singular "magic bullet," but there are a number of strategies that can help.

First, *prioritize.* Remember the research that found 79% of employees who leave voluntarily cite a lack of appreciation as a primary reason they quit? Take that to heart. If you have key team members whom you don't want to lose, you better *make sure* they feel valued. If you don't, they will eventually be looking for another place to work. Find out how your "stars" like to be shown appreciation and make a point of doing it the way they would prefer. Secondly, if you know some of your colleagues are worn out or discouraged,[4] it would be wise to do something to encourage them. Find out their primary language of appreciation, and what actions they value, and reach out to them. (Appreciation and encouragement are largely the same actions but with a different time focus. Appreciation is directed toward the past—what they've done that you value. Encouragement is focused on the present and future—coming alongside and encouraging them to persevere and keep going.)

> If you have key team members you don't want to lose, you'd better make sure they feel valued.

A second strategy is to *delegate.* As we have said throughout the book, supervisors and managers *cannot* provide all the encouragement and appreciation needed. This is especially true when you are responsible for a large team. Try to find a lead employee who gets the importance of showing appreciation to others, and bring them alongside you to share the responsibility in modeling appreciation and looking out for those who need encouragement. Better yet, form a small group of team members who want to become the "lead cadre" in appreciation and determine specific team members they will focus on.

Thirdly, **take bite-sized actions.** Don't try to eat the "whole hog" at once; take one bite at a time over time. Don't attempt to set up a big, overarching program or draw up a spreadsheet where you (and even your appreciation partners) try to reach everyone on the team in the next month. Do a little here, a little there. As you do, you will become aware of all of the opportunities there are daily to communicate a little appreciation to someone (even if it isn't in their primary appreciation language!), and you will become more adept at doing so effectively. Also, when your colleagues see that you are trying to communicate appreciation, they often will become more willing to take a step themselves in showing appreciation to their coworkers.

Start somewhere with someone.

Are there challenges in effectively showing individual appreciation when you work with a large group? Absolutely. But don't let the challenge prevent you from doing what you can. As we repeatedly emphasize: *Start somewhere with someone.* You will get a better result than doing nothing at all.

Q4: HOW CAN APPRECIATION BE USED WITH VOLUNTEERS?

In the United States and around the world, hundreds of thousands of organizations utilize volunteers every week. The breadth and span of their impact seems virtually immeasurable. The biggest challenge that most organizations who utilize volunteers have is the fact that volunteers tend to be "short term." Many volunteers work for an organization for a few weeks or months, then fade away and discontinue their service.

If you analyze the reasons that people continue to volunteer, they fall into two categories: *social connectedness* and *perceived impact*.

When volunteers feel connected to others—those they are serving, their coworkers, and the staff of the organization—the longevity of their commitment increases dramatically. Conversely, we know that when volunteers feel isolated from others, when they don't feel supported by staff members, and when they don't feel relationally connected to those they are serving, they will quit.

Most volunteers also want to "make a difference." They want to know that what they are doing is important and is having a positive impact on others. The problem is, many volunteer efforts do not make significant and visible differences immediately. Therefore, volunteers can't always see the impact of their service. It is critical for their supervisors and support staff to help them see how their service fits into the big picture, and how it will make a difference over time. Volunteers need input and perspective from their supervisors in order to understand the impact they are truly having.

HOW APPRECIATION MAKES A DIFFERENCE

In bolstering volunteers' sense of both social connectedness and perceived impact, the role of the supervisor and the encouragement of colleagues are exceedingly important. Effectively conveying your appreciation for the work they are doing in ways that are meaningful to the volunteer can significantly boost volunteer retention.

We have found that organizations that take the time to find out how their volunteers are best encouraged and that discover their primary languages of appreciation (through using the *MBA Inventory*) have far more success in "hitting the target" with their volunteers. Supervisors also have communicated that they are amazed at how much less time and energy it takes to encourage volunteers when they know what will encourage that person, versus putting on large appreciation events that miss the mark for many of their workers.

If you are an administrator of a nonprofit organization or a supervisor of volunteers, consider this: Wouldn't it be helpful to write notes and give verbal thanks to those individuals for whom it really matters? Wouldn't it be delightful to give a small number of gifts to those who appreciate them, and to know what gift they would like? Think of the amount of time and energy you could save if you spent time individually or in small groups with those who value quality time. Wouldn't it reduce your anxiety to know which volunteers value and are motivated by working together and which are fine with working independently?

One of the most common complaints by volunteers about attempted displays of appreciation is that it feels like "one size fits all." Our internal research shows that public recognition is one of the least favorite forms of receiving appreciation. Yet this is a favorite practice of nonprofit administrators when they give the "volunteer of the year" award or have the chairperson of the fundraising event stand up and receive recognition. Unfortunately, organizers of these events don't understand that they may be actually causing damage in their relationship with this key person, rather than rewarding them.

An obstacle to showing appreciation to volunteers in the ways meaningful to them is the cost of having volunteers take the *MBA*

Inventory (while low in cost to virtually every other work-based assessment, many nonprofits feel they do not have the money to fund the assessments). We have found that when leaders of non-profit organizations communicate to their Board of Directors the negative impact of high turnover and the cost of retraining volunteers, often funds are "found" (sometimes in the form of being underwritten by some of the Board members).

We believe that when organizational leaders understand the 5 languages of appreciation and their importance to retaining volunteers, they are then able to be far more effective in their efforts to express authentic appreciation to their volunteers and keep them connected to the organization.

Q5: HOW DO PERSONAL LOVE LANGUAGES RELATE TO THE LANGUAGES OF APPRECIATION?

People who are familiar with *The 5 Love Languages®* and have gone through the process of identifying their own preferred love language in personal relationships are often curious about the relationship between the two sets of languages. We are frequently asked, "What is the relationship between a person's personal love languages and their languages of appreciation? Are they identical? Are they somewhat related? Or are they totally different?"

We can say, then, that in general the ways people experience and prefer acts of encouragement, appreciation, or affection would be similar over time and many settings. But we would also predict that there is a good chance for many people that how they relate to others, and how they prefer others communicate appreciation to them, would change in response to who the other person is and the type of relationship they have.

The second source of understanding the relationship between personal love languages and languages of appreciation in the workplace comes from the years of experience we have had in working with these concepts. Clearly, one of us (Gary) has more experience in the context of the love languages within personal relationships, while the other (Paul) has had more focus on work-based relationships and the languages of appreciation. We both independently came to the same conclusion: over time we would find out that there is a moderate correlation and overlap between individuals' preferred languages, regardless of the setting or type of relationship. But we also expect that there would not be an exact overlay, and there will be variation both across most preferred and least preferred languages. This is, in fact, what we have found.

Clients and individuals who have gone through training sessions with us consistently report that they believe that, for themselves, there is a general overlap across their languages of appreciation in the workplace and their personal love languages, but it is not 100 percent. For example, Betsy, a lead teacher in a middle school, stated, "Receiving verbal praise is important to me in either setting. So it is one of my top two languages on both scales. But quality time with my husband is far more important and comes out higher on the five love languages scale."

Similarly, Chris, the comptroller for a corporation, said, "I think I'm basically the same person whether I am at work or at home, but clearly there are expressions of affection I value from my wife that I don't look for from my colleagues at work. So I would expect my preferred languages to differ in those two relationships."

In a study with adjunct faculty at a university, we found that only 38% of the participants had the same primary language on both the *MBA Inventory* and the five love languages profile. So for the majority of this group, their primary languages weren't the same. However, when looking at the results more closely, we found the following: 69% of the faculty members had their primary love language as either their first or second highest language of appreciation. That is, if Quality Time was their highest love language, then Quality Time was either their first or second preferred language of appreciation. And the results were essentially the same when going the other direction. If verbal praise was an individual's highest language of appreciation, then 67% of the time Words of Affirmation was either their first or second highest love language.

The bottom line: your "love languages" and "languages of appreciation" won't always be one and the same—but most of us will have some commonalities between the two.

CHAPTER 14

HOW APPRECIATION WORKS IN DIFFERENT SETTINGS

WE HAVE BEEN EXCITED TO see the positive results experienced by thousands of work groups when applying the concepts of the 5 languages of appreciation in a wide variety of organizations. The success of helping leaders and employees from various types of organizations learn how to communicate authentic appreciation seems to be the result of three factors:

1. The need for feeling valued and appreciated is universal.
2. The 5 language concepts are easy to understand, learn, remember, and apply.
3. The principles can be customized (seemingly) to

virtually any type of work setting. (We haven't found a work setting yet where authentic appreciation doesn't work!)

As we have worked with hundreds of companies and organizations across the world (and have hundreds more certified facilitators using our materials in twenty-six countries), we have approached the process with a learning attitude. Yes, we firmly believe the foundational concept of communicating authentic appreciation in the ways meaningful to the recipient is solid and true. But we also know that each work setting (even within a company or similar industries) has its own unique characteristics. As a result, the concepts need to be implemented in the ways that match each workplace culture.

We understand and are committed to this process of "tweaking" the *Appreciation at Work* training to fit the needs of each workplace. Hence (we believe) our success. We don't try a cookie-cutter approach to use the same training process or ways to communicate appreciation in every setting. We have developed several specific versions of the *MBA Inventory* designed to match the actions one would find in a variety of work settings.[1] For example, an appropriate Act of Service will look different in a public school setting than in a hospital surgical ward or in a government social service agency.

We have put together a number of examples of how the 5 languages of appreciation have been applied to different industries. (For further specific stories shared by leaders and additional examples, see the chapter "Unique Settings" in *The Vibrant Workplace.*)

MANUFACTURING FIRMS

We were told by one business consultant that "This appreciation stuff is too 'touchy-feely'" to work in the manufacturing sector. Another business owner said, "Supervisors and line workers on the floor don't care about feelings. They just want to get the job done and get their paycheck."

What we have discovered, however, is that there are owners of manufacturing firms who understand the need to show appreciation to their team members, and who are actively looking for a model that will work within their organization. When the business leader understands the potential benefits and they find a practical model they can apply to their setting, they become visionary leaders and put the ideas to work within their company.

> "People will do almost anything for you because they know you care about them personally."

One such company, a small firm that manufactures and assembles electrical components, had us take their leadership team through the *Appreciation at Work* process. When the team reported their experiences, one director commented, "You know, it has been my experience over the years that when you communicate appreciation to your team, it creates a sense of loyalty. People will do almost anything for you because they know that you care about them personally. I think good managers understand this. But this gave me the specific information I need on *how* to encourage my people."

FAMILY-OWNED BUSINESSES

Family-owned businesses include a wide variety of endeavors: construction companies (residential, commercial, and highway), dry cleaners, restaurants, auto dealerships, manufacturing companies, car washes, real estate management companies, heating and air-conditioning contractors, banks—the list is virtually endless. Also, family-owned businesses range in size from a few employees to tens of thousands globally.

As noted earlier, over 85 percent of all businesses in the United States are family-owned. Thirty-five percent of Fortune 500 companies are family businesses. In fact, family-owned businesses employ 60 percent of all employees in the nation.

To the surprise of those who don't work with family businesses, family members are often the ones who feel the *least* appreciated of all employees. This seems to be a common experience, perhaps because others see them as part of the ownership and conclude that they don't need to be encouraged.

One family member confided to us: "No one understands the pressure I feel. No matter what I do, it is not good enough for my dad. The nonfamily employees think I have it 'made' financially. In reality, I make less money than most of the other managers and receive no distributions from the company. If I could leave, I would, but it would destroy my relationship with my family and I don't want to do that." This woman needed to know she was valued by the other employees in the company, including her parents.

It is also our experience that business owners are one of the loneliest groups in the workforce. Given both their position and their entrepreneurial personality, business owners rarely receive much communication of appreciation from their employees. Many owners have concluded that "this is the way it is" and no longer expect appreciation from their employees. So, if you are an employee, even if your boss looks like he or she is doing fine, we would strongly encourage you to take the time and effort to communicate gratitude for all they do for the business.

SCHOOLS

Schools at every level of education are experiencing tremendous pressures. In fact, we believe that schools are one of the most difficult environments in which to work in today's society. Teachers and educational professionals face demands from all sides— meeting federal and state testing standards, dealing with students with learning difficulties and behavioral problems, coping with everyday classroom and academic challenges. Add a myriad of other issues with which to contend—stressed parents, divorce conflicts, and chaotic home environments—and you have a cauldron for burnout and discouragement.

Combine these factors with the declining funds available for resources, decaying physical facilities, and lack of pay increases for all staff, and the result is a work environment in which employees struggle with high demand and little tangible reward. This is the type of setting in which consistently communicating appreciation is vital for staff and teachers so that they do not lose heart and become discouraged.

One elementary school principal reported, "It is critical for me to know how to specifically encourage my teachers in practical ways. I can't give them a raise, but I can do things to help them feel that what they are doing is important and noticed."

An inner-city middle school administrator, when he found out about the *MBA Inventory,* became excited because it dovetailed with a program his district was launching. After first utilizing the inventory with his administrative team, he then had his lead teachers take the questionnaire and use the results in their weekly staff meetings. The team members were skeptical initially but warmed up over time as they realized the model was not one of manipulation but focused only on communicating *authentic* appreciation.

College settings are also ripe for appreciation-focused managing. In fact, over 700 colleges and universities have used our resources. These institutions tend to be massive bureaucracies with territorial battles occurring regularly. There are also very clear hierarchies, and the organizational culture is often very competitive. As a result, the organizations are not very warm interpersonally, and positive, supportive communication between colleagues can be rare. Administrators who communicate gratitude and appreciation to their staff members quickly become effective supervisors.

NONPROFIT ORGANIZATIONS

Many nonprofit organizations provide direct services (American Red Cross, Habitat for Humanity, Salvation Army, and many others). Others serve within their local communities—for example, organizations supporting the arts. These organizations face the constant need to make the community aware of their presence and mission, and have an ongoing need to raise funds. Staff members within these groups need continual encouragement and appreciation.

This can be challenging. While those who work for nonprofit organizations often have a sense of calling and are motivated by a sincere desire to serve others, they still need to feel appreciated. Nonprofit staff members often earn significantly less than they would in the for-profit sector. Nonprofit organizations are not known for paying huge salaries. In these work settings, the need for appreciation is critical in keeping the staff energized.

Many nonprofit organizations are underfunded, and the demands on the organization's staff are significant, often overwhelming. We have worked with a variety of social service organizations: a residential treatment facility for adolescent males with severe behavioral problems, a community counseling clinic for low-income families, an inner-city mentoring program for father-less children, and a number of church-based organizations. All of these organizations are doing good work in providing valuable and needed services to their clientele. However, they are often difficult places to work, with high demands, low resources, and not much external recognition from the community. As a result, the burnout rate for staff (and volunteers) is high. Fortunately, the *Appreciation at Work* model works extremely well in these nonprofit settings.

FINANCIAL SERVICES

Some may think that those who work in the financial services industries (insurance, investment advisory services, and banking) would not need the *Appreciation at Work* model. They believe that individuals who work in this arena are primarily motivated by financial reward. While this may be true for the professional advisors themselves, their support team members need consistent encouragement as they work in a demanding, often high-pressure work environment.

We have consulted with the highest producers in a number of the national life insurance groups. One of the most common concerns voiced has been: "How do we keep our staff? They get frustrated with us and leave after twelve to eighteen months. The turnover rate is killing us." In meeting with the office staff (separately from the financial professionals), we found that office managers, receptionists, administrative assistants, and back-office technicians often are starved for appreciation from their bosses. This is partially due to the fact that their team members feel appreciated in different ways than they do.

We have found that 50–60% of administrative support staff members adamantly do *not* want to be recognized publicly for doing a good job. Yet their bosses repeatedly attempt to show appreciation in this way—and totally miss the mark.

Accountants are realizing the need within their profession to deal with the relational aspects within their job settings. In fact, the governing bodies of Certified Public Accountants have validated that emotional intelligence skills are critical to the success of the accounting profession. As a part of the training model for these skills, the "best practices" model for CPA firms includes the admonition to "encourage people to build a network of support and encouragement."[2]

MEDICAL/DENTAL OFFICES

Medically related professional practices tend to be very receptive to the 5 Languages of Appreciation model. Hospitals, dental and orthodontic offices, outpatient physical therapy clinics, optometry practices, and a wide range of medical service businesses repeatedly tell us, "We need this!" We have helped to implement *Appreciation at Work* in large hospital systems, large multisite practices, and small, single-office settings.

One medical office we worked with shared positive results. One supervising physical therapist reported, "This has been a very beneficial experience for us. Although we were already a positive place and we tell each other 'Thank you' a lot, going through this process reinforced and enhanced what we were already doing." Another therapist said, "It seems like appreciation is now a part of who we are. We have all started to show appreciation more often and regularly. It has become a part of our culture."

MINISTRIES AND CHURCHES

Employees of churches and other ministries often have a unique relationship with their vocation. Their job is a source of income, but they also bring to their work a sense of calling and a desire to serve others. In many church settings, employees are expected to give of themselves sacrificially, which almost always includes a lower salary than they would receive doing similar work in a different setting.

> In our research on toxic workplaces, we sadly found churches and ministries to be overrepresented.

In our work with church staff members and individuals who work for other nonchurch ministries, we consistently find a deep hunger for appreciation. These people are not looking for financial reward and rarely desire high levels of praise. But they honestly express the need to be appreciated for their time and efforts. When appreciation is not forthcoming, they often become discouraged. In fact, in our research on toxic workplaces, we sadly found churches and ministries to be overrepresented, "missing the mark" in their efforts to show appreciation.[3]

LAW ENFORCEMENT, GOVERNMENT, AND MORE

We have had significant interest from government agencies at all levels—local, state, and federal. These are work environments where there is little room for financial incentives or promotion based on one's performance. As consumers of services provided by these agencies, we often see the discouragement and apathy displayed by governmental employees. We developed a unique version of the *MBA Inventory* for government employees and have seen a major impact in numerous settings by improving the work environment and daily experience of these individuals.

The need for encouragement and appreciation is also being communicated within law enforcement leadership circles. In his article in *Law and Order*, Robert Johnson argues that the ability to establish a personal connection with people separates effective leaders from mere administrators. He states, "While awards are nice, officers need the emotionally sincere expression of heartfelt approval and appreciation for a job well done. . . . When they sometimes make a questionable decision and they beat themselves up about it, they need encouragement, not judgment."[4]

Research has already been done in hotel and restaurant management that demonstrates the need for teams to learn authentic appreciation. More than three decades of research has shown that managers' style of leadership and behavior accounts for more than 70% of employees' perceptions of organizational climate. In fact, employees' feelings about management were found to be the main factor that improves employees' perceptions of their company's organizational climate. Successful managers develop and improve face-to-face communication with employees; they show care for and respect to employees by expressing appreciation and gratitude and encouraging and facilitating teamwork.[5]

GLOBAL APPLICATION

The need for appreciation and encouragement is not limited to the United States or English-speaking nations. We have been utilizing the *Appreciation at Work* model both internationally and with a variety of multinational organizations. *The 5 Languages of Appreciation in the Workplace* has been translated into seventeen languages and our resources have been used in more than sixty countries.[6] Additionally, we have translated the *MBA In-*

ventory into Spanish, French, Chinese, Danish, Norwegian, and Hungarian.

We are excited about the opportunities to help managers, supervisors, and coworkers in creating more positive work environments in a wide range of industries and around the world!

Making It Personal

1. *In your work, what is your greatest challenge?*

2. *What is there about your work that gives you the deepest sense of satisfaction?*

3. *If you struggle to stay motivated on your job, what causes you the deepest sense of discouragement?*

4. *How do you think understanding the languages of appreciation could enhance your work environment?*

CHAPTER 15

DOES A PERSON'S LANGUAGE OF APPRECIATION EVER CHANGE?

WHEN WE WORK WITH COMPANIES, we're often asked, "Does a person's primary language of appreciation ever change—either over time or in certain circumstances?"

The answer to this question is yes. A person's preferred way of being shown appreciation *can* change. But we believe (and have observed) that most individuals' primary appreciation language tends to be quite stable. The ways in which we prefer to be shown appreciation at work seem to largely remain similar across time (sort of like a baseline we keep returning to), but variations can occur due to situational factors.

We are in the process of investigating this issue. As might be expected, however, finding out how stable (or varying) our appreciation languages are over time *takes time to figure out*. We are examining this question by having groups of individuals retake the *MBA Inventory,* some over short time periods (weeks) and others over a longer timeframe (years). The longer the timeframe between taking the assessments, the more likely other factors may play a part as well—whether or not the individual is at the same job, at the same workplace but in a different position, has a different supervisor, and so on. And, like any general statement about groups of people, there will almost certainly be individual differences.

Let's explore two factors we have observed that affect the primary ways individuals like to be appreciated.

LIFE CIRCUMSTANCES AND LIFE STAGES

First, one's current **life circumstances** can influence how one wants to be supported and encouraged. When an individual is going through a stressful time, the ways in which they feel valued often change. The situation may be a medical problem they personally are experiencing, having to cope with the declining health or death of an aging parent, stress due to behavioral or academic challenges of a teenager, or having to consider a job change due to external factors affecting their company. During these times, we are all "stretched to the max," burdened with demands on our time and emotions.

Emotional support and encouragement are critical during these times, from family and friends *and* from colleagues at work (since that is where many adults spend the majority of their waking hours). We have found that, during these intense times of life, our preferred language of appreciation may shift.

Generally, Quality Time and Acts of Service become more prominent during times of stress. Why? Because, in most cultures, spending time with others who are hurting and doing some practical actions to make their life easier are two common ways we care for one another. Quality Time may be demonstrated by listening to a coworker share the logistical challenges they are facing in trying to care for their mother who is failing mentally and physically. An Act of Service may involve covering for your teammate in a conference call, so they can go to a meeting with their child's principal to address a concern.

"I WILL NEVER FORGET WHAT YOU'VE DONE FOR ME"

Michael is a hardworking CPA in a large accounting firm. When he first took the *MBA Inventory*, his primary language of appreciation was identified as Words of Affirmation. Michael agreed with this assessment. What really made him feel appreciated was when people recognized his work and verbally affirmed him.

Six months after Michael took the inventory, his wife was diagnosed with cancer. The next two years involved frequent trips to the doctor, two surgeries, and chemotherapy. During this time, Michael's colleagues at work gathered around and strongly supported him. Two female coworkers would stay with Michael's children so he could accompany his wife to her medical appointments. Two other employees arranged to take meals to Michael's home after each of his wife's surgeries.

Michael later said to these four coworkers, "I will never forget what you have done for me. I could not have made it without your help." To this day, he looks back on that experience as one of the times when he felt most deeply appreciated by his colleagues. During that season of Michael's life, the language of Acts of Service spoke more deeply to him emotionally than Words of Affirmation. When we looked at his *MBA Inventory*, we noted that Acts of Service was his secondary language of appreciation. But during this intensely personal crisis, his secondary language became his primary language. So, life circumstances can temporarily affect our preferred language of appreciation.

Secondly, the specific "action steps" within one's preferred appreciation language also may shift with *different stages of life*. Bryan is a sales manager for a manufacturing firm. In his mid-thirties, he frequently travels to see potential customers and as part of doing business goes out to dinner at fairly nice restaurants with them. Earlier in his adult life, like many young couples, Bryan and his wife, Sandi, lived on a pretty tight budget, so eating out was a rare treat. At that point in his career, Bryan and Sandi would have welcomed a gift card to a nice restaurant as a demonstration of appreciation for his good work. However, at this stage a gift card to a restaurant would have less value to Bryan, even though his primary appreciation language is Tangible Gifts. Now, since he and Sandi have developed an interest in music, they prefer concert tickets. This is an example of how the specific action desired within an appreciation language may change over time and in various life stages.

Or consider Michelle, a top performer in a national sales organization. Her primary language of appreciation is Words of Affirmation. When she received her first public recognition as "salesperson of the month," she called her mother and told her about her success. She even read the words on the award that she received. She felt genuinely affirmed and appreciated. Four years later, Michelle's closet is filled with awards and plaques that she has received for various accomplishments. She now takes it all in stride and seldom shares the award with her mother or anyone else. She simply puts the plaque in the closet and moves on to her next accomplishment.

Recently her supervisor stopped by her office and said, "Michelle, I have given you more plaques and awards than anyone in the history of the company. I could give you another plaque if you like. But I wanted to stop by personally and let you know how much I appreciate your contribution to the company. Not only are you a great salesperson, but you also motivate others. In many ways, you are the most significant person in our sales force. I want you to know that I sincerely value your contribution to the company. Next week, if you don't object, I'll give you another plaque. But I just wanted you to know that, with me, it's not just the perfunctory giving of an award, but I sincerely appreciate what you are doing." Michelle thanked her supervisor for his comments. When he left the office, tears came to her eyes and she said to herself, "I believe he really does appreciate my efforts."

While Words of Affirmation is Michelle's primary appreciation language, it was the fact that her supervisor took the time to come by her office and verbally express his appreciation that spoke deeply to her. This was more effective than the public recognition in front of her colleagues. Her supervisor spoke both the language of Quality Time and Words of Affirmation.

How can you tell when an appreciation language changes?

So how do you know when a person's primary language of appreciation may have changed for a season or that their action steps have shifted in importance? Sometimes you can observe it by simply acknowledging their present circumstances. Michael's colleagues were aware of his wife's illness, and those closest to him knew what would help and responded instinctively. They were not thinking, "What is Mike's appreciation language?" They were thinking, "What could we do that would be helpful in this situation?" But in so responding, they communicated appreciation to Michael in the deepest possible way. Sometimes if we are simply in tune with our colleague's life circumstances, we will be able to intuitively know what help would mean the most.

On the other hand, Bryan's supervisor or colleagues may not have known that a gift card to a nice restaurant was no longer as meaningful to him as it had been earlier in his life. The fact that Bryan preferred a ticket to a concert rather than a gift card to a restaurant would have to be communicated to his supervisor and colleagues. That is why we encourage those who take the *MBA Inventory* and list their "action steps" to revisit these action steps semiannually and provide new information as to ways that might make them feel appreciated. If this can be worked into a semiannual review by the supervisor, it makes it much easier for the employee.

The influence of interpersonal dynamics

Allow us to think like psychologists for just a moment. In the early days of psychology (from the early 1900s through the 1970s), the focus of psychotherapists was primarily on individuals—their personality characteristics, behavior patterns, habits, and how they thought. However, eventually psychologists became aware that an individual's behavior occurred within a context—within a system (of relationships) rather than in isolation. This led to the development of what is called Systems Theory. The basic idea is that people's behaviors and thoughts are best understood if you understand the system in which they live. This discovery led to the development of marriage and family therapy and social psychology. It sought to give a more thorough understanding of how one's social context changes one's behavior. An obvious example is how a teenager greets her friends versus how she greets her grandmother.

The key point of this discussion for our purposes is that a person's primary language of appreciation may shift, depending on the person to whom they are relating. For example, what they desire from a colleague may differ somewhat from what they desire from a supervisor. The personality of the supervisor may also affect what the employee would like to receive as an expression of appreciation. In exploring this issue, it is evident that our languages of appreciation, while residing primarily in "who we are," are also influenced by the characteristics of the person with whom we are interacting.

> A person's primary language of appreciation may shift, depending on the person to whom they are relating.

This interpersonal dynamic impacts our language of appreciation as well. Consider this example. Tonya generally values compliments and other verbal expressions of appreciation; this is her primary appreciation language. However, Tonya's current supervisor is a high-energy marketing professional. Glenn is a dynamic individual who showers positive comments on virtually everyone he meets. "What a great day! How is it going, Joseph? I sure appreciate the work you got done for me yesterday. You did a super job!" And on he goes to the next team member.

People love Glenn because he is so encouraging. However, because he offers so much verbal praise, it can somewhat diminish its perceived value by those close to him. So when Glenn compliments Tonya, she is grateful but also tends to discount the message somewhat.

What really makes an impact on Tonya is when Glenn stops

by her office and asks not only how things are going but also what suggestions she has that might enhance the performance of the department. When he stops long enough to have a conversation with her, she senses that he sincerely appreciates her efforts and insights. She knows that Glenn is fast-paced and always on the go. He rarely sits still for extended conversations. He is often interrupted by phone calls, text messages, or people wanting to talk with him. To his credit, he responds quickly to those who are contacting him, but Glenn can also be rather distracted. In the middle of a conversation, he can think of someone he needs to call and does so immediately. "Hold that thought," he may say. "I need to call Kevin about something real quick. It will only take a second." Thus, when he takes time to not only verbally affirm Tonya but also listen to her ideas, she senses his sincerity.

Interestingly, Quality Time is Tonya's secondary language of appreciation. But in relationship with Glenn, it clearly becomes more important than her primary appreciation language. Therefore, although her *MBA Inventory* results would communicate to Glenn that Tonya values verbal affirmation, in actuality her primary way of receiving encouragement from Glenn is to have a quality conversation in which he gives her his undivided attention. Because of the personal dynamics, Tonya's primary language from Glenn has shifted from Words of Affirmation to Quality Time.

Who is going to know this shift in languages? Tonya. Over time, if she pays attention to her internal responses, she will become aware that what she really desires from her supervisor is Quality Time. So, it will be important for her to clarify this both for herself and to Glenn.

There is one other factor that is illustrated by Tonya's experience. When a person receives an adequate supply of their primary language of appreciation, their secondary language may then become more important. Tonya's primary language of appreciation is Words of Affirmation. That's who she is. But inasmuch as Glenn gave an abundance of words of affirmation, it had become less important, and Quality Time became more meaningful. Our guess is that if Glenn stopped giving her verbal affirmation on a regular basis, her primary language of appreciation would quickly revert to Words of Affirmation.

Or consider Tim's situation. He is a hard worker, with high expectations of himself. However, because of the nature of his job and the fact that the company has downsized, he sometimes becomes overwhelmed with the quantity of work expected of him. On the *MBA Inventory*, his primary language of appreciation was Acts of Service. When colleagues pitch in and help him with a project, he genuinely feels appreciated. And yet Tim has one colleague whose help he does not appreciate. This colleague is an incessant talker, while Tim is a rather quiet person. When the colleague is helping him, he is talking and joking and telling stories constantly. Tim finds this very distracting and annoying. He cannot give his attention to his own work while his colleague is attempting to help him. Therefore, because of the personal dynamics in their relationship, Tim's primary language with *this* colleague is not Acts of Service. If this colleague offers to help him, he will now say, "No thank you. I've got it covered. Thanks for asking."

We hope these illustrations help clarify the impact of personal dynamics on one's language of appreciation. The remaining question is, "How would Tim's talkative colleague know that Acts of Service is not the primary appreciation language that Tim would like to receive from him?" Our suggestion is: Before assuming you know what a person's primary language is, ask, "Would this be helpful to you?" If their response is, "No thank you. I've got it covered," and you get this response at least twice, then you can assume that their primary language of appreciation *from you* is not Acts of Service.

CONCLUSION

The point we are trying to make in this chapter is that, even though you seem to have a baseline appreciation language you typically prefer, you should not be surprised if you discover that your primary language of appreciation shifts in certain circumstances and with certain people. Nor should you be surprised to discover that the same may be true of your colleagues.

We encourage you to be aware of your own internal reactions and the responses of your colleagues. Life is not static; people and their lives change over time. We believe the best managers are those who know their people well, continue to get to know them, and make appropriate changes as needed.

All this points to the importance of regularly checking in with your team. As a part of these proactive evaluations, you can easily discover any changes in their primary and secondary languages of appreciation or the action steps that they would prefer.

Making It Personal

1. Can you remember circumstances in your own life when your primary language of appreciation seemed to shift? What were the circumstances that stimulated this shift?

2. *If you have experienced a painful personal event in your life, how did your colleagues support you during that time? Did you find their support to be meaningful?*

3. *If you have seen a shift in your primary language of appreciation or the action steps you would like to receive from others, how might you communicate this information to those with whom you work?*

4. *Can you identify personal dynamics between you and a colleague that lead you to conclude that you prefer a different type of appreciation from them (than from others with whom you work)? What type of appreciation is more meaningful from this individual? Why do you think that might be the case?*

CHAPTER 16

OVERCOMING YOUR CHALLENGES

THE QUESTION IS NOT, "Do you appreciate your coworkers?" The real question is, "Do they *feel* appreciated?"

We've looked at ways to do that in this book. However, we must admit that it is not always easy to make your team feel appreciated. If communicating appreciation and encouragement to those we work with was simple, then everyone in the company would be a happy camper. There would be no need for this book or for a structured approach to motivating by appreciation. The truth is, there are challenges that get in the way of effectively expressing gratitude to our colleagues. Some are internal issues—attitudes, thoughts, and beliefs. Other challenges are external and relate to corporate structures and procedures.

These challenges need to be faced realistically, but they can be overcome. Here are some of the common challenges and our suggestions on how to solve them as you seek to create a positive work climate.

CHALLENGE #1: BUSYNESS

In the work we have done with organizations, the most frequent reason given (by far) that appreciation is not a regular part of communication is the *busyness of the team members*. Almost everyone feels stretched in their daily responsibilities. Who is sitting around trying to figure out what to do with all of their extra time? Not many of the people we have met.

But workers must have the mental space to observe others if they are going to appreciate what their team is doing. They also must possess the emotional energy to consider and plan the best way to express appreciation to a particular colleague. Without available mental, physical, and emotional space, nothing will change.

Overcoming busyness[1]

The most important way to overcome busyness is to prioritize. Some things *are* more important than others. If the most important things do not take priority, then our time and energy invested in other matters will fail to produce the desired results.

We highly recommend Steven Covey's classic leadership books *First Things First*[2] and *The 7 Habits*

Some things *are* more important than others.

of Highly Effective People.[3] These books provide a helpful process to aid leaders and team members to identify those priorities that are most important to them and make them a part of their daily and weekly routine. If our priorities are not reflected in our schedule, then they cease to be priorities. Covey's quadrant of priorities—important/not important, urgent/not urgent—has been helpful to each of us in our personal and professional lives.

We believe that for supervisors, business owners, and managers, giving time and energy to show appreciation to your colleagues and those who work for you is an important task that will yield large dividends in your organization and the services you provide. However, for many team members, expressing appreciation is usually not urgent, and if you do not intentionally plan to do it, the non-important but seemingly urgent matters of the day can crowd out the daily discipline of communicating appreciation to your team.

CHALLENGE #2: THE BELIEF THAT COMMUNICATING APPRECIATION IS NOT IMPORTANT FOR YOUR ORGANIZATION

Some organizational leaders hear about the languages of appreciation and immediately say, "I can see how that would be good in some companies, but it won't work in my industry. Manufacturing workers aren't big into saying thanks or caring about how others feel." We have heard similar comments from a variety of business leaders in the areas of finance, sales organizations, Fortune 500 corporations, restaurant chains, auto repair shops, and various other work settings. Interestingly, the results of research paint a different picture. Almost all research indicates the positive impact of nonfinancial rewards on the lives of workers in almost every industry.[4]

What we have found is that the type of business or organization really is not an important factor. The real issue is the mindset of the owner, director, or supervisor. If leadership does not feel that appreciation is important, they are not likely to see the need for expressing appreciation to those who work for them. If this mindset is not changed, then their employees are forced to live in a thankless community, wishing that things could be better.

Overcoming the "Appreciation won't work in my organization" attitude

As we have discussed, we have discovered that in reality, the *Appreciation at Work* model can be successfully utilized in virtually any organizational setting, regardless of how hard-nosed or financially driven the culture may be. The most important variable is that a leader or supervisor understands the power of individuals feeling valued for the work they do and the contributions they make toward the organization's success.

For each leader who has reacted negatively, we have had other leaders in the same industries who recognized almost immediately the value of employees feeling appreciated. When they hear of the *MBA Inventory* and the concept of individualizing expressions of appreciation, they are eager to get started. We have seen leaders in traditionally "tough guy" industries (mining, trucking, the military) who have chosen to include appreciation as a part of the organization's culture. Increased employee engagement, lower turnover rates, and higher ratings of job satisfaction have followed.

One corporate executive changed his mind. The first time he heard about the concept, he said, "I don't really care about how my people feel about their work. They are driven individuals who are motivated by potential financial success, and we set up a system to reward them in that way." Later, after his industry had a major financial downturn, he came back to us, saying, "If there is a way to encourage and motivate our employees without paying them more, I'm all for it. How can we get started?"

In a world where employees are often expected to do more work for less pay, learning to express meaningful appreciation may make the difference between failure and success for the company.

CHALLENGE #3: FEELING OVERWHELMED WITH EXISTING RESPONSIBILITIES

When working with the volunteer staff of a nonprofit organization, one of the team members blurted out, "I'm all for this appreciation stuff and I think it is a great idea. But just thinking about keeping track of my team's languages of appreciation and their action steps overwhelms me. It's all I can do to keep up with my current responsibilities." Her openness and candor was important to us, and we expressed our understanding of the stress she was feeling.

Feeling overwhelmed is more than being busy; it also includes the sense of weighty responsibility. Some individuals can easily feel overloaded when discussing communicating appreciation to their colleagues. They feel that expressing appreciation to coworkers is just another responsibility added to their plate. If pressured to participate in the process of learning to express appreciation in meaningful ways, these individuals can become very negative and disgruntled. That is why we always encourage companies to let participation in the *Appreciation at Work* training be done on a voluntary basis.

> Feeling overwhelmed is more than being busy; it also includes the sense of weighty responsibility.

Overcoming the "overwhelmed" feeling

This is going to sound awfully "psychologist-like," but the first and best response you can give to a team member who is feeling overwhelmed is to *acknowledge and validate their perspective.* Do your best therapist imitation and say, "Boy, it sounds like you are really feeling overwhelmed." Then listen with concern as they expound further on their feelings.

Conversely, telling them, "Oh, come on. It's not that big of a deal. We are just asking you to do what you are already doing," generally doesn't make things better. Ignoring their sense of exasperation and moving on with the plan usually leads to resistance or resentment.

In some situations, after venting their feelings, and feeling heard by their manager, some employees say, "It really isn't that big of a deal; I can do this. I guess I just needed to vent. I really do want my coworkers to feel appreciated." In other situations, the person is reacting to what they think they heard, not really what you attempted to say. It is especially important to emphasize that encouraging their team members is not the sole responsibility of supervisors, but is an "everyone is responsible" process. This clarification can reduce resistance significantly.

However, other members may need you to give them the option to not pursue this plan at this time. As noted above, in working with organizations, we propose that participation in the process should be voluntary and not a top-down directive. This strengthens the perception that the actions individuals choose to take to encourage others are genuine. Their efforts to validate coworkers are not seen as something they were "supposed to do."

Additionally, sometimes the timing isn't right. Members of a team want to learn how to support and encourage one another but now is not a good time (e.g. fiscal year end for the accounting department). We encourage leaders and departments to choose the right time for working together to implement the concepts within their team.

CHALLENGE #4: STRUCTURAL AND LOGISTICAL ISSUES

When working with one office team, we were following up with encouraging emails to the team members. One of the staff responded to an email by saying, "I am trying to encourage Jenna but I just haven't seen her this week. We're working different shifts with little overlap of time, and when we are together we are generally working in different areas. So I don't have much opportunity for interaction with her."

Sometimes there are logistical issues that interfere with the process of sharing appreciation for others. Varying schedules, few natural opportunities for interaction, working on different projects, and nonmatching vacations often make it difficult to express appreciation to certain coworkers.

There can also be structural challenges to overcome. Those who work in larger corporations point out that some managers are responsible for 20 or more direct reports. Obviously, the larger the number of people for whom you are responsible, the greater effort it will take to keep up with their individual languages of appreciation—and to find the time to do so.[5]

Sometimes a business is structured such that a team member actually has two or more supervisors. This happens most often when their responsibilities cross departmental boundaries. Although it is fine for more than one supervisor to encourage this worker, the situation may create a vacuum when no one takes the responsibility to encourage the worker at all.

Overcoming structural and logistical issues

Structural issues can be one of the more difficult challenges to overcome because they often are embedded in the fabric of the organization. They are not just individual issues but more systemic in nature. The answer may require supervisors and higher-level managers to work together in finding a solution. The real question that needs to be answered is, "How can we best ensure that Chantel is consistently encouraged and shown appreciation? Who is the most logical person to provide this type of communication and feedback to her?"

The answer to this question takes the discussion outside of "who reports to whom." Finding the team member who has the opportunity to observe and give encouragement to Chantel, and from whom she would value receiving this type of communication, is the more important issue.

In situations where a manager supervises a large group, we have found success in helping the manager identify one or two people with whom they will start the process. Later, they can move to other team members. The employees can be selected either because they are key leaders for the unit and losing them to discouragement would be devastating to the organization, or they may be workers who are clearly currently discouraged or disconnected from their supervisor and need immediate attention. Picking one or two people to start encouraging is clearly a better option than feeling overwhelmed and not doing anything at all.

CHALLENGE #5: PERSONAL DISCOMFORT WITH COMMUNICATING APPRECIATION

We see this in two forms. The first is the age-old position of some business owners and managers: "Why should I thank them for doing their job? That is why I pay them." We find this attitude sometimes comes from senior leaders and other individuals who view themselves as self-made leaders. They were raised through difficult circumstances, often with little family support, and have become successful in their field largely due to hard work, perseverance, and personal grit. These leaders are tough-minded and typically don't have a lot of focus on relationships or feelings. They view responsibility as a primary virtue and they don't look to others for thanks or appreciation. They do what they do because "we are supposed to," or "that's just what you do." Thus, they tend to hold little value for showing appreciation of any kind to others.

A variation of this position is found among driven young professionals. We have experienced resistance from bright, hard-working Gen X and millennial professionals. One such young woman commented to us, "I am self-motivated, and I always do my best. I don't expect to be praised for doing my job, and I think this whole process is irrelevant."

The second version of personal discomfort in communicating appreciation comes from individuals who have difficulty communicating on a personal level. These leaders and managers often are fact-oriented and task-driven. They are all about "getting the work done" and are often excellent supervisors in the area of production. These individuals usually don't show much emotion aside from anger and frustration when goals are not being met. Sometimes they can be pleasant and congenial, but their focus is on "just the facts, ma'am." They find it difficult to express appreciation to colleagues. If they do so, it may come across in a very matter-of-fact manner. Often their comments are brief: "Thanks." "Good job, Amanda." "Nice work, Marcus." Then they move on to the next goal to be achieved.

These employees often don't have a wide range of emotional expression. They are appreciative but just don't think of sharing their thoughts or feelings with others. Therefore, unless prompted to do so, they rarely express appreciation to coworkers.

Overcoming personal discomfort

Employees who don't seem to intrinsically value showing appreciation to their colleagues may never change their viewpoint. Some people have their mindset and are not open to exploring new ideas. To try to force this person to change is likely a waste of time and energy, and to do so will only result in frustration.

However, some of these individuals are willing to listen to facts. Research has shown numerous benefits to organizations and their team members (see chapter 2). Once they see that we are talking about *authentic* appreciation (and not "going through the motions" recognition), these leaders are willing to enthusiastically support building a climate of expressing appreciation in their organization.

Other leaders may be willing to "do an experiment," even if only to prove you wrong. We believe that if a work group will take the *MBA Inventory* and share the results with one another, a significant number of individuals will start to apply the information and begin to create a more positive work environment.

> For employees who are less socially skilled to successfully show appreciation to their colleagues, they need to start with "baby steps."

A second group of persons who express discomfort are those who are more introverted, less socially skilled, or not as relationally oriented. For these individuals, the task is to find the acts of encouragement and appreciation within the general parameters of their comfort zone. These team members often need more structure, more encouragement, and monitoring to make sure that they actually follow through. For them to successfully show appreciation to their colleagues, they need to start with "baby steps"—those actions that clearly fall within their current repertoire of behavior. They need to be praised and encouraged for any action that approximates the desired behaviors.

We have had success in working with high-tech companies and employees,[6] learning the unique ways they like to be shown appreciation.[7]

CHALLENGE #6: THE "WEIRDNESS FACTOR"

One of the interesting challenges we have encountered in working with businesses and organizations on the languages of appreciation is what we have come to call the "weirdness factor." This "weirdness" comes from the fact that everyone in the room is hearing the material on how to encourage and show appreciation to one's colleagues, and they are each working on a plan to implement the concepts in their daily work relationships—with one another! Many times at this point someone in the room says, "I'm with you on the need to do this, and I want to start using what you have taught us. But it feels kind of weird because we're all going to start encouraging one another and doing things to help out our teammates—but we all know it's part of this training. So it can feel sort of fake." And usually, most of the people in the room are nodding in agreement.

Two issues need to be addressed here. First, there is the discomfort of starting to relate somewhat differently to one's colleagues, with everyone knowing that the impetus comes from the languages of appreciation concepts and training. This often leads to a hesitation in starting to communicate appreciation or encouragement for fear of being perceived as fake or disingenuous. "They're going to think I'm just doing this because I'm supposed to—that they're just a project to me," is a comment we sometimes hear.

The second part of the "weirdness factor" is the risk of the recipient dismissing another's act of encouragement as not being genuine, or that they are doing it to "look good in front of the boss." If people aren't careful, they can question the sincerity of their colleagues' intentions.

So then a sense of weirdness is created internally both within the individual who is *initiating* an act of encouragement and within the person who may *receive* a message of appreciation. The combination of these two thought patterns, if left unaddressed, can be deadly to the process—no one does anything for fear of their actions being judged as not being authentic and genuine.

Overcoming the "weirdness factor"

We have found some very simple steps that can be taken that can greatly diminish the weirdness factor. First, *we acknowledge it.* As part of the process of developing action steps for each team member, if the issue hasn't come up, we bring it up. "You know, we have found that many times as we begin to talk about these ideas, people start to feel a bit weird about everyone working on encouraging one another at the same time." You can actually see and feel the level of anxiety in the room decrease significantly. (In psychological circles, this is called "normalization"—helping people realize that what they are experiencing is normal enables them to accept their situation and reactions more readily.)

Secondly, *we relate the experience to previous life experiences.* Whenever people try something new or different, the new behavior can feel a bit odd or unnatural. It doesn't "flow" initially. (There are lots of examples—learning to dribble a basketball, adjusting one's golf swing, changing one's wardrobe or hairstyle, beginning an exercise program with a trainer.) We encourage people to understand and accept the initial strangeness, but also to persevere and work through it—it usually goes away fairly quickly.

We also provide tools to get past the weirdness. It can be as simple as giving the team a sample sentence such as, "I know you may

think I am doing this just because of the languages of appreciation training we have been doing, but I really do . . ." Putting the
concern out front usually disarms the issue. And we also encourage the use of humor to defuse the situation. When a person is
a recipient of an act of encouragement, and it is obvious to both
parties that it has flowed from their training, we've encouraged
team members to say something like, "Thanks, I feel *so* much better now—like I am valued and appreciated" (with a smile, not a
sarcastic tone). There usually is a lot of laughter that occurs when
colleagues begin to use the various languages of appreciation and
the specific action steps from their teammates' list.

Finally, *we encourage everyone to give the benefit of the doubt to
their coworkers and accept their actions as being genuine.* Let's be
honest: it takes courage to take a new idea and try to make it work
within your daily work relationships. When a colleague tries to
communicate appreciation, having a receptive attitude and thinking, "Hey, at least they are trying; I appreciate the effort," leads to
positive interactions all around.

In fact, later in the training process, we repeatedly hear comments like, "I have to tell you, at first I thought this whole process
was kind of weird—a bit 'touchy-feely' for me. And at the beginning, even though I knew my colleagues were saying things and
doing things because it was part of this project, it still felt really
good. I liked hearing the nice things they had to say."

CONCLUSION

We would be intellectually dishonest if we were to claim that applying the 5 languages of appreciation is an easy process for every
individual and in every setting. This is clearly not the case. There
are some workers for whom encouraging colleagues will be a

significant "growth-point." Some work settings have intrinsic characteristics that make communicating appreciation more difficult.

However, we have not found a company or nonprofit organization for which the *Appreciation at Work* process concept cannot work. The challenge often requires some creative thinking and problem solving, but the problems have never been insurmountable.

Making It Personal

1. On a scale of 0–10, to what degree is busyness a hindrance to your implementing the concept of Appreciation at Work? If busyness is a major problem for you, would you consider trying to make effective expressions of appreciation one of your priorities for the next two months? (And then evaluate the results you are seeing.)

2. On a scale of 0–10, how strongly do you feel that the 5 languages of appreciation would enhance the work climate of your organization? If you are strongly motivated, then what will you do to encourage others to join you in this pursuit? If you feel it will not work, would you be willing to discuss the concept with at least one of your colleagues and get their opinion?

CHAPTER 17

WHAT IF YOU DON'T APPRECIATE YOUR TEAM MEMBERS?

"BUT WHAT IF I DON'T REALLY appreciate those who work for me?" one organizational leader asked us. Our first thought was that he was joking, but then he said, "No, really; what am I supposed to do if there are people on my team that I don't appreciate? I'm not pleased with the work they're doing. Should I just go ahead and try to communicate appreciation to them?"

Our first and immediate response was, "No! If you don't appreciate a team member, don't try to fake it. That will almost assuredly undermine the relationship further."

We have found that there are both internal and external reasons for lack of appreciation of team members. The internal reasons reside within ourselves while the external reasons are various factors in the work setting that make it difficult for us to feel appreciation toward a specific colleague. First, let's examine the internal issues.

SORTING OUT OUR OWN ISSUES

We may have unrealistically *high expectations* of our team, expecting more than they are capable of performing. Thus, no matter what a person does, it is not "good enough" for us. We are not pleased with the end product. We may criticize or make suggestions of how the task could have been done better, quicker, or more cheaply.

Some individuals who have high expectations of others are driven people who are often quite successful. These people may be business owners, managers, colleagues, customers, or vendors. Because they are driven, they naturally drive others and can sometimes be quite overbearing.

On the other hand, some people who have high expectations for others simply have a critical personality. They are not necessarily successful themselves. In fact, they may overestimate their knowledge and skills. They have developed a lifestyle of criticizing others. These people will never have good relationships for one simple reason: no one likes to be constantly criticized.

If you find yourself dissatisfied with the performance level of a number of people who work under your supervision, it would be wise to take an honest self-assessment and see if you have unrealistically high expectations. If you quickly answer, "No, I just have high standards," you may be rushing to an inaccurate conclusion. We suggest that you ask a friend who will be honest with you this question: "Do you think that I have unrealistic expectations of others? Please give me your honest opinion." If your expectations are indeed unrealistic, you will never become an encourager because no one can please you. There is only one answer: you must revise your expectations so that you can genuinely appreciate the hard work of those you supervise.

A second internal factor is the reality that *some people just rub us the wrong way*, and this can happen in the workplace. We react negatively to someone, not because they aren't doing their job but because they *irritate us*. The irritation might stem from some aspect of their personality. In your opinion they may "talk too much" or "they can't carry on a conversation." It may be that their work space always looks disorganized, or you may resent the fact that they consistently show up for work ten minutes late and leave ten minutes early. Perhaps you are annoyed that they seem to always be happy. You can't believe that anyone could be that happy all the time. Conversely, you may say to yourself, "Every day they look like their best friend just died."

> Some people just rub us the wrong way, and this can happen in the workplace.

The irritation may also come from the way they do things. The way they approach a task is exactly the opposite of the way you approach the same task. You may resent the fact that they like to listen to music while they work. The earbud in their ear makes you think they are not giving their full attention to their work. Every time you see it, you get irritated. Or perhaps you get irritated because of the way they dress. In your opinion, their dress is inappropriate for their job.

Sometimes it's simply that the person's lifestyle is different from your own. You can't imagine why they would wear rings in their nose or have tattoos on their arms or a hairstyle that, to you, is barbaric. Sometimes it is generational differences that irritate us. The middle-aged single mother is disturbed by the young "macho" single male who acts like the world revolves around him.

There are many things that may spark personal irritations. This is true in all human relationships. The reality is, people are different. In the work setting, the question is, "Are they performing their job in a satisfactory manner?" If the answer is yes, then you can genuinely express appreciation to them for their work even though you may be irritated by other issues. If the answer is no, and you are the supervisor, then you need to address the problem of work performance.[1]

The truth is we cannot change individuals' personalities and lifestyle patterns so that everyone looks and acts like us. We have to accept human differences and look for ways to encourage those whose behavior may get under our skin but whose work performance is positive.

A third reason some supervisors have difficulty expressing appreciation is that they have *inadequate information.* We have found some supervisors do not appreciate team members whom they do not directly supervise because they don't fully understand the individual's responsibilities. There is a lack of information resulting from poor communication patterns within the organization.

"SHOULDN'T CHRIS BE IN HIS OFFICE?"

One supervisor, Rob, said, "I don't get what Chris does. All I see him doing is flitting here and there, going from one office to another. I thought he was our IT guy. Shouldn't he be in his office making sure the computer system works correctly?"

Sasha, the director of information systems, responded to Rob, "Chris is our network specialist and his first responsibility is to make sure that each person's computer is hooked up to the computer network properly so they can communicate with everyone else. The reason you see him going place to place is because he is responding to calls for help from people whose computers aren't working correctly. He goes to see them personally, hears what their problem is, and fixes it. He is doing exactly what he is supposed to do. And he is doing it well."

"Ohhh. Okay, if that is what he is supposed to be doing— great!" Rob replied, somewhat sheepishly.

If you have a question about the work performance of someone who does not work under your direct supervision, it is always wise to talk to the person to whom the employee reports. You may find that your concern is simply due to lack of information. When Rob encountered Chris in the hallway two days later, he said, "Chris, I hear good things about your work from Sasha. I appreciate your efforts to make everyone's computer work correctly." Chris walked away feeling affirmed. Rob was able to express genuine appreciation because he took time to get information.

Now let's turn to external issues.

IF THE ISSUE IS PERFORMANCE

Often, we find that a manager is not pleased with a person on her staff for good reason. It is not related to some internal thought pattern on the part of the manager. There are practical reasons behind the manager's lack of appreciation for the colleague. The employee may not be performing the job adequately. This happens in almost every organization. Some individuals simply are not doing their jobs at an acceptable level of quality.

There may be many reasons for this lack of performance. First, many people do not perform satisfactorily because *they have not been adequately trained for their responsibilities.* In our experience, we have found this is a common reason for low performance on the job. The supervisor either assumed the employee had the skill and knowledge base, or believed they would pick it up on their own. In a few weeks or months, colleagues notice that the employee is not completing the task on a satisfactory level. This reality often goes unobserved by the supervisor because she assumes that the human resources department has adequately screened new employees. However, few employees arrive on the scene with all the skills and information needed to adequately perform their jobs.

> Few employees arrive on the scene with all the skills and information needed to adequately perform their jobs.

When a supervisor or manager realizes that the person does not have the information or training necessary to perform the job, the most positive response is to provide the training. In today's world, most employees are willing to take training opportunities in order to keep their job. Once a manager sees the person taking the initiative to learn and consequently raising their performance level, the manager can then honestly give authentic appreciation to the employee. In this case, the employee feels encouraged and motivated to continue reaching their potential on the job.

Another common reason for low job performance is that the organization *does not have in place an effective process for review, feedback, instruction, and correction.* In our work with businesses, one of the most common deficits we observed is the lack of established processes for reviewing employees' performance, giving them regular feedback, and providing corrective instruction. This is a formula for frustration, both for the team member and supervisor.

All of us have "growth areas." Supervisors and team members need regular times to communicate with each other about what is going well and what can be improved. When there is not a structured process in place, this type of communication often does not occur.

Third, the employee may have *physical problems*. Employees who live with chronic pain, are not sleeping well, or have a medical condition that may not be readily apparent to others, may not be performing at their typical capability level. We have found that frequently (for a variety of valid reasons) individuals tend to be private about any physical ailment they are experiencing, even when it is obvious that something is affecting their work performance.

Additionally, the employee may have *personal problems at home*. It is well known that when people are going through a divorce, their performance on the job is adversely affected. When adults are struggling with the illness of an aging parent, it can be very distracting. Parents who have a child struggling in school or a teenager "acting out" may find it difficult to keep focused on their work.

Or some employees may simply have a *low work ethic*.[2] They have developed an approach to work that is, "Only do what is necessary." They may be enduring the job in order to keep food on the table.

A manager has no way of knowing what is underlying poor performance unless the manager talks with the employee. Many managers do not like confrontation and will go for months avoiding the issue of a low-performing employee. Unfortunately, this does not resolve the situation, and the manager becomes increasingly frustrated. Such a manager will have a hard time expressing appreciation to this employee.

Our suggestion is that the manager should have an open, honest conversation with the individual. The approach needs to be kind but straightforward. You might say something like this: "Jen, I have observed in recent weeks that you have not been performing to your potential on the job. This concerns me. I know there is probably an explanation, and that is why I wanted to talk with you. Is there something going on in your life that is contributing to your decreased performance? If so, I want to do anything I can to help you." Such a caring approach will likely bring the manager an honest answer.[3]

With this information, the manager can then be helpful to the employee. One manager who had such a conversation with an administrative assistant discovered that the employee's son was on drugs. She was able to help the employee find an affordable treatment program for her son and in the process deepen their friendship and increase the employee's productivity. Then the manager was able to express authentic appreciation. The administrative assistant then reciprocated appreciation to the manager.

CONCLUSION

We have already noted how employees can see through insincere appreciation. In fact, we openly encourage supervisors not to attempt communicating appreciation if they truly do not appreciate the team member. Going through the motions of communicating appreciation when there is not a genuine basis for it will do real harm to the relationship between the supervisor and the team member.

It is far better to wait—and deal with the root issues. If the supervisor realizes that the problem is an issue within herself, then she must identify what is keeping her from giving genuine appreciation. On the other hand, if the supervisor concludes that the issue is one of the three external factors that we have discussed, she must provide more training for the employee, seek to establish a regular process of giving corrective feedback to the individual, or directly address the personal issues of the team member.

One final note. Given the myriad of issues related to how (or whether) to communicate appreciation when you are struggling to truly appreciate a colleague, we explore and address the issues more deeply in *The Vibrant Workplace: Overcoming the Obstacles to Building a Culture of Appreciation.*

Making It Personal

1. *Are there individuals you work with that you find it difficult, if not impossible, to express authentic appreciation to? What factors seem to be related to this challenge for you?*

2. *Do you think you may be difficult to appreciate for some of your colleagues? If so, what issues may be relevant?*

CHAPTER 18

NOW IT'S YOUR TURN

COMMUNICATING APPRECIATION and encouragement to one's fellow workers is a powerful tool in influencing your organization positively—regardless of your position within the system. We are well aware, however, that the ability and willingness to show appreciation and communicate encouragement is not a magic bullet that will solve all of the challenges within a workplace.

We acknowledge that a healthy work environment will be characterized by a number of factors, including:

- Quality team members
- Effective communication skills and procedures set in place to facilitate regular communication
- Trusting relationships
- Common vision and goals among team members
- Standardized processes and procedures, including standards to be met and ongoing monitoring of performance
- Healthy methods for correction and conflict resolution

- Clear lines of responsibility, including accountability and rewards for results

The more these characteristics exist in an organization, the more likely the organization will meet its goals and the team members will enjoy their work.

We also know that no organization is perfect. Each has its own unique strengths and weaknesses.[1] But we have found that when the members of an organization engage in communicating appreciation and encouragement in the ways that are most meaningful to their team members, then good things happen:

- Relationships between supervisors and employees, and between coworkers, improve.
- Tardiness and absenteeism decline.
- Team members become less irritable and touchy.
- Interactions between colleagues take on a more positive tone.
- Quality team members (including volunteers) stay with the organization longer.
- Customer satisfaction ratings rise.
- Employees (and managers) report that the workplace environment becomes more enjoyable.

APPRECIATION, VITAMINS, AND ANTIBIOTICS

Let us share with you a word picture that we have found helpful to illustrate the power of encouragement and appreciation in transforming work-based relationships. The consistent use of encouragement (coming alongside a team member and encouraging them to persevere) and appreciation (communicating a sense of value for the work they have done and the character qualities they demonstrate) are a lot like vitamins and antibiotics.

Both are chemicals that help our physical bodies maintain health. Taking vitamins regularly is a proactive habit that provides the building blocks for developing healthy bodies. When a wound has occurred, antibiotics are chemical compounds that fight off an infection. Both have their place in keeping our bodies healthy.

Some interesting characteristics should be noted about vitamins and antibiotics. First, the chemicals that make up vitamins and/or antibiotics are typically not so powerful that one dosage meets the need the body has (there are some very strong antibiotics, but these are the exception rather than the rule). Taking a vitamin (or even a host of them) once really will not affect your physical system much. Their power and influence are a result of a series of small actions occurring consistently over time. Faithfully taking a daily multiple vitamin over a long period of time can help provide the chemicals that you need to develop a healthy body. Similarly, when an infection is developing, the repeated use of an antibiotic is needed to heal the wound or condition.

Second, different people need a variety of elements in varying amounts to maintain health. There is not a "one size fits all" multivitamin supplement that meets everyone's needs. Some people need more calcium; some need more iron; others need fairly obscure trace minerals. And there is not just one antibiotic that is suited to kill all the bacteria that can create infections. A topical antibiotic can help a skin cut heal, while another type of antibiotic is needed to fight strep throat. And it is critical to use the right chemical in the right situation. If we don't, the body doesn't get the nutrients or support it needs to be healthy.

Finally, vitamins and antibiotics are not dramatic. It can be easy to forget to take your vitamin or apply the antibiotic to a

When appreciation and encouragement are consistently communicated over a long period of time, in ways that are important to the individual, the impact can be dramatic.

wound. And missing a day or two probably won't hurt you significantly. But if you consistently and repeatedly forget to take the vitamins you need, or stop taking your antibiotic as prescribed, over time the health of your body will almost certainly be affected negatively.

So it is with appreciation and encouragement. A single act of encouragement doesn't look like it is going to change the world or make a real difference in a colleague's life. But when appreciation and encouragement are consistently communicated over a long period of time, in ways that are important to the individual, the impact can be dramatic. And when an organization is composed of healthy parts communicating effectively, and when a physical system is equipped with defenses to fight off unhealthy invaders, it can mean the difference between surviving difficult times and succumbing to a general lack of health.

APPLYING THE CONCEPTS IN *YOUR* WORKPLACE

Regardless of your position within your organization, you can make a real difference in their workplace by beginning to encourage and show appreciation to your colleagues. We have seen individual employees in a variety of roles (frontline employee, supervisor, manager) start "where they are," include one or two colleagues, and then have their supervisor become intrigued, explore our resources, and begin to take their team through the *Appreciation at Work* process. In fact, frequently organizations will engage in a pilot project where they have a small team of employees interested in learning how to show authentic appreciation to one another. They try out the concepts, others see how well the process works, and appreciation begins to spread throughout the organization. To assist individuals and organizations in applying the 5 languages of appreciation, we have created a wide range of resources and tools for small groups to large multinational organizations.[2]

No matter your role or the type of setting in which you work, you can start to impact those around you by beginning to communicate appreciation to those with whom you work on a daily basis. The key is to start *somewhere* with *someone.*

KATHY: "I THOUGHT I KNEW MY TEAM MEMBERS"

Let us share one final example. As a district supervisor for an international social service agency, Kathy was aware of the need to develop a leadership training process for her key leaders across a three-state region. Given that the organization was nonprofit, the team members were there largely out of a sense of calling to serve others. Although her team was generally healthy, she knew that they were at risk for burning out due to the ongoing demands of the work they did and the limited resources of the organization. Through a leadership training course Kathy was taking, she became aware of the *5 Languages of Appreciation in the Workplace* project. She felt that her leaders needed encouragement and support, but she sensed that she was not hitting the mark in her efforts.

We arranged to do an introductory session via videoconference for her team members who were spread across a number of offices. We introduced the *Appreciation at Work* concepts to the team and had each of the team members (approximately ten) take the *MBA Inventory*. We conducted a follow-up video-conference to go over their results to more fully explain the languages of appreciation in daily life, and helped them develop initial action plans for implementing the process. We shared with her team members a group chart showing each individual's primary language, secondary language, and least important language. We continued to follow up with email reminders and suggestions for them to try, every two weeks for three months.

The results were significant. Kathy shared with us that knowing how to specifically encourage her team members greatly enhanced her efforts at expressing appreciation. She also developed a list of the preferred action items for each of the team members' primary languages of appreciation. This gave her team specific information on how best to express appreciation to team members.

Later Kathy said, "I thought I knew my team members and what was important to them, since we had worked together a number of years. However, I realized that I was off base with a number of them. Having them identify their preferred languages of appreciation and especially including the specific action items important to them has made it far easier for me to hit the mark, even across long distances."

She continued, "The changes in our team are remarkable. We get along better and genuinely appreciate each other more. I am seeing the team members reach out and encourage others when they see someone struggling. It has become a 'fun thing' for us—learning how to effectively communicate appreciation."

While we were working with Kathy, she was promoted to a new supervisory position of a larger district. Kathy told us, "I am going to use the *MBA Inventory* with my new team. There is a huge need. The relationships aren't as healthy—a lot of internal competition with some bickering. They need help and tools in how to communicate more positively with one another. I can't wait to see what's going to happen. Let's get going!"

GET GOING!

Communicating appreciation and encouragement effectively isn't rocket science. The ideas are not that hard to understand intellectually. The key to success, like with most behavioral change, is to actually *start* to apply the concepts, "get back on the horse" when you fail to keep working the plan, and be committed to persevering over the long haul. Then you will see the positive benefits of your efforts.

We believe that the desire to work (engaging in meaningful, productive activity—whether paid or not paid) is innately in the nature of being human. And the experience of enjoying one's work comes from a combination of factors: our own attitudes, practicing healthy habits within relationships, being affirmed and valued by others, and acknowledging that enjoying one's work is a gift given by our Creator.

It is our desire that myriads of employees and volunteers will find the concepts of this book to be a significant tool to help them create a more positive workplace. We believe that enhancing the emotional climate in an organization helps the organization more effectively reach its goals. If people enjoy their work and feel appreciated by supervisors and colleagues, they are far more likely to have organizational loyalty and work hard to help the organization continue to be successful.

By effectively communicating appreciation and encouragement to others, you can be the impetus that creates a more positive work environment for yourself and those around you.

NOTES

INTRODUCTION

1. Mike Robbins, *Focus on the Good Stuff: The Power of Appreciation* (San Francisco: Jossey-Bass, 2000), 32.

CHAPTER 1: *WHAT EMPLOYEES WANT MOST*

1. Stephen Covey, *The 7 Habits of Highly Effective People Restoring the Character Ethic* (New York: Free Press, 2004), 241.
2. Go to www.mbainventory.com to learn about the various versions available.
3. Marcus Buckingham and Donald O. Clifton, *Now, Discover Your Strengths* (New York: Free Press, 2001) 171.
4. Tony Schwartz, "Why Appreciation Matters So Much," Harvard Business Review, 2012, https://hbr.org/2012/01/why-appreciation-matters-so-mu.html.

CHAPTER 2: *FOR BUSINESS LEADERS: WHY APPRECIATION IS A GOOD INVESTMENT*

1. See the chapter, "Can Appreciation Cross Cultures?" in Paul White, *The Vibrant Workplace: Overcoming the Challenges to Building a Culture of Appreciation* (Chicago: Northfield Publishing, 2017).
2. Rodd Wagner and James K. Harter, *12: The Elements of Great Managing* (New York: Gallup Press, 2006).
3. Glassdoor Team, "Employers To Retain Half Of Their Employees Longer If Bosses Showed More Appreciation; Glassdoor Survey," Glassdoor, November 13, 2013, https://www.glassdoor.com/employers/blog/employers-to-retain-half-of-their-employees-longer-if-bosses-showed-more-appreciation-glassdoor-survey/.
4. Sylvia Vorhauser-Smith, "How the Best Places to Work Are Nailing Employee Engagement," Forbes, August 14, 2013, https://www.forbes.com/sites/sylviavorhausersmith/2013/08/14/how-the-best-places-to-work-are-nailing-employee-engagement/#143ab6e65cc7.
5. John R. Darling, Michael J. Keeffe, and John K. Ross, "Entrepreneurial Leadership Strategies and Values: Keys to Operational Excellence," Journal of Small Business & Entrepreneurship 20, no. 1 (January 2007): 41–54, https://doi.org/10.1080/08276331.2007.10593385.

6. Fred Luthans et al., "Positive Approach To Leadership (PAL) Implications for Today's Organizations," *Journal of Leadership Studies* 8, no. 2 (September 14, 2001): 3–20, https://doi.org/10.1177/107179190100800201.

7. Wagner and Harter, *12: The Elements of Great Managing*.

8. Kevin Kruse, *Employee Engagement 2.0: How to Motivate Your Team for High Performance: A Real-World Guide for Busy Managers* (Richboro, PA: The Kruse Group, 2012), 6.

9. Wagner and Harter, *12: The Elements of Great Managing*.

10. James K. Harter et al., "The Relationship between Engagement at Work and Organizational Outcomes," Gallup, February 2013, http://employeeengagement.com/wp-content/uploads/2013/04/2012-Q12-Meta-Analysis-Research-Paper.pdf, 2.

11. Wagner and Harter, *12: The Elements of Great Managing*.

12. "Top 12 Employee Appreciation Statistics," *Baudville* (blog), 2015, https://ideas.baudville.com/the-baudville-blog/top-12-employee-appreciation-statistics.

13. Leigh Branham, *The 7 Hidden Reasons Employees Leave: How to Recognize the Subtle Signs and Act Before It's Too Late* (New York: AMACOM, 2005), 3.

14. Timothy A. Judge et al., "The Relationship between Pay and Job Satisfaction: A Meta-Analysis of the Literature," *Journal of Vocational Behavior* 77, no. 2 (October 1, 2010): 157–67, https://doi.org/10.1016/J.JVB.2010.04.002.

15. Martin Dewhurst, Matthew Guthridge, and Elizabeth Mohr, "Motivating People: Getting Beyond Money," McKinsey Quarterly, 2009, https://www.mckinsey.com/business-functions/organization/our-insights/motivating-people-getting-beyond-money.

16. Vivian Giang, "The Strengths And Weaknesses Of Millennials, Gen X, and Boomers," Business Insider, BusinessInsider.com, 2013, http://www.businessinsider.com/how-millennials-gen-x- and-boomers-shape-the-workplace-2013-9.

17. Kathy Gurchiek, "What Motivates Your Workers? It Depends on Their Generation," SHRM.org, May 9, 2016, https://www.shrm.org/resourcesandtools/hr-topics/behavioral-competencies/global-and-cultural-effectiveness/pages/what-motivates-your-workers-it-depends-on-their-generation.aspx.

18. Sami Abbasi and Moncef Belhadjali, "A Closer Look at Millennials at Work: A Literature Review," *International Journal of Humanities and Social Science Review* 2, no. 4 (2016): 17–19.

19. Gurchiek, "What Motivates Your Workers? It Depends on Their Generation."

20. Abbasi and Belhadjali, "A Closer Look at Millennials at Work: A Literature Review."

21. Edward L. Deci, Richard Koestner, and Richard M. Ryan, "A Meta-Analytic Review of Experiments Examining the Effects of Extrinsic Rewards on Intrinsic Motivation.," *Psychological Bulletin* 125, no. 6 (1999): 627–68, https://doi.org/10.1037/0033-2909.125.6.627.

22. Vorhauser-Smith, "How the Best Places to Work Are Nailing Employee Engagement."

23. Darling, Keeffe, and Ross, "Entrepreneurial Leadership Strategies and Values: Keys to Operational Excellence."

24. Luthans et al., "Positive Approach To Leadership (PAL) Implications for Today's Organizations."

25. Victor Lipman, "66% Of Employees Would Quit If They Feel Unappreciated," Forbes, April 15, 2017, https://www.forbes.com/sites/victorlipman/2017/04/15/66-of-employees-would-quit-if-they-feel-unappreciated/#21333bff6897.

26. Sami M. Abbasi and Kenneth W. Hollman, "Turnover: The Real Bottom Line," *Public Personnel Management* 29, no. 3 (2000): 333–42, http://sites.jmu.edu/wp-content/blogs.dir/774/files/2016/10/Public-Personnel-Management-2000-Abbasi-333-42-1.pdf.

27. Jac Fitz-enz, "It's Costly To Lose Good Employees," *Workforce*, August 1, 1997, http://www.workforce.com/1997/08/01/its-costly-to-lose-good-employees/.

28. Rudy Karsan, "Calculating the Cost of Turnover," *Employment Relations Today* 34, no. 1 (2007): 33–36, https://doi.org/10.1002/ert.20139.

29. Karlyn Borysenko, "What Was Management Thinking? The High Cost of Employee Turnover," TLNT: Talent Management & HR, 2015, https://www.tlnt.com/what-was-leadership-thinking-the-shockingly-high-cost-of-employee-turnover/.

30. Branham, *The 7 Hidden Reasons Employees Leave.*

31. Lipman, "66% Of Employees Would Quit If They Feel Unappreciated."

32. Stacia Sherman Garr, "The State of Employee Recognition in 2012," Bersin & Associates, June 2012, http://go.achievers.com/rs/iloverewards/images/analytstinsights-the-state-of-employee-recognition.pdf..

33. Bruce Tulgan, "The Great Generational Shift: Update 2018," 2018, http://rainmakerthinking.com/assets/uploads/2018/01/Gen-Shift-2018.web_.pdf.

34. Kronos Incorporated, "The Employee Burnout Crisis: Study Reveals Big Workplace Challenge in 2017," Kronos, January 9, 2017, https://www.kronos.com/about-us/newsroom/employee-burnout-crisis-study-reveals-big-workplace-challenge-2017.

35. WorldatWork, "Trends in Employee Recognition," May 2017, https://www.worldatwork.org/resources/surveys/trends-in-employee-recognition.

36. Dan Schawbel, "What Employers Will Worry About in 2017," *Fortune*, December 28, 2016, http://fortune.com/2016/12/28/employers-2017-employee-retention-unemployment/.

37. Branham, *The 7 Hidden Reasons Employees Leave.*

38. For a thorough examination of the challenges associated with traditional recognition programs, see chapter 10: "The Difference between Recognition and Appreciation," and also chapter 3: Paul White, *The Vibrant Workplace: Overcoming the Challenges to Building a Culture of Appreciation* (Chicago: Northfield Publishing, 2017).

39. Nicole Stewart, "The Power of Appreciation: Rewards and Recognition Practices in Canadian Organizations," The Conference Board of Canada, June 2017.

40. Ibid.

41. Mark Goulston, "What to Do When Praise Makes You Uncomfortable," Harvard Business Review, December 13, 2013, https://hbr.org/2013/12/what-to-do-when-praise-makes-you-uncomfortable.

42. Intellective Group, "Incentive Marketplace Estimate Research Study," 2016, http://theirf.org/research/incentive-marketplace-estimate-research-study/1836/.

43. Paul White, "How Do Employees Want to Be Shown Appreciation? Results from 100,000 Employees," *Strategic HR Review* 16, no. 4 (2017): 197–99, https://doi.org/10.1108/SHR-06-2017-0037.

44. Nicole Stewart, "The Power of Appreciation: Rewards and Recognition Practices in Canadian Organizations," The Conference Board of Canada, June 2017, 36.

45. Rex Huppke, "Top Workplaces Winners Find Ways to Incorporate Gravy," *Chicago Tribune*, November 12, 2013, http://www.chicagotribune.com/business/ct-xpm-2013-11-12-ct-biz-tw-assurance-benefits-20131112-story.html.

46. Rainer Strack, "Decoding Global Talent: 200,000 Survey Responses on Global Mobility and Employment Preferences," Boston Consulting Group, 2014, https://www.bcg.com/en-us/publications/2014/people-organization-human-resources-decoding-global-talent.aspx.

47. Baudville Blog, "Top 12 Employee Appreciation Statistics."

48. SHRM/Globoforce, "SHRM/Globoforce Employee Recognition Survey," Fall 2012, http://go.globoforce.com/rs/globoforce/images/SHRMFALL2012Survey_web.pdf.

49. Janice Kaplan, "GRATITUDE SURVEY Conducted for the John Templeton Foundation June-October 2012," 2012. https://greatergood.berkeley.edu/images/uploads/JTF_GRATITUDE_REPORTpub.doc.

50. Tim Wolock and Chris Martin, "The Formula for a Winning Company Culture," 2016, https://www.payscale.com/data/employee-engagement.

51. Paul White, "Online 'Train the Trainer' Program," Appreciation at Work, 2011, https://www.appreciationatwork.com/train.

52. See chapter 10 for a thorough discussion on the differences between appreciation and recognition: *The 5 Languages of Appreciation in the Workplace: Empowering Organizations by Encouraging People*.

53. Paul White, *The Vibrant Workplace: Overcoming the Challenges to Building a Culture of Appreciation* (Chicago: Northfield Publishing, 2017).

54. See Paul White, "APPRECIATION AT WORK RATING SCALE™," 2011, https://www.appreciationatwork.com/aawrs/.

CHAPTER 3: APPRECIATION: FROM BOTH MANAGERS AND PEERS

1. See chapter 10: "The Difference between Recognition and Appreciation" for more information.

2. For more information on millennials, see chapter 13: "Generational Differences and Other FAQs."

3. "The Effect of Work Relationships on Organizational Culture and Commitment," Globoforce, Fall 2014 Report, http://go.globoforce.com/rs/globoforce/images/Fall_2014_Mood_Tracker.pdf.

4. SHRM/Globoforce, "SHRM/Globoforce Employee Recognition Survey," Fall 2012, http://go.globoforce.com/rs/globoforce/images/ SHRMFALL2012Survey_web.pdf.

5. Ibid.

6. Go to www.appreciationatwork.com/train to see the resources available.

CHAPTER 4: *APPRECIATION LANGUAGE #1: WORDS OF AFFIRMATION*

1. We have explored the relationship between individuals' primary language of appreciation and Myers-Briggs: Paul White, Natalie Hamrick, Tim Hepner, Rob Toomey, "How Personality Type and Languages of Appreciation Interrelate," www.appreciationatwork .com/learn.

2. A code for taking the inventory is included inside the back cover of this book. Go to www.mbainventory.com to purchase registration codes for your colleagues.

CHAPTER 5: *APPRECIATION LANGUAGE #2: QUALITY TIME*

1. Paul White, "Don't Hire Your Clones: Diversity in Practice," Human Talent Network, 2015, https://www.humantalentnetwork.com/dont-hire-your-clones-diversity-in-practice/ 7595/#content-anchor.

2. Jennifer Ellis, "Best Practices in Volunteer Management: An Action Planning Guide For Small and Rural Nonprofit Organizations Acknowledgments," 2005, http://www .volunteeryukon.ca/uploads/general/Best_Practices_Volunteer_Management.pdf.

3. Rob Asghar, "What Millennials Want In The Workplace (And Why You Should Start Giving It To Them)," Forbes, January 13, 2014, https://www.forbes.com/sites/ robasghar/2014/01/13/what-millennials-want-in-the-workplace-and-why-you-should-start-giving-it-to-them/#305e4ea44c40.

4. Ernst & Young LLP, "Younger Managers Rise in the Ranks: Survey Quantifies Management Shift and Reveals Challenges, Preferred Workplace Perks, and Perceived Generational Strengths and Weaknesses," 2013, http://www.ey.com/Publication/vwLUAssets/EY-Survey_ shows_younger_managers_rising_in_the_ranks/$FILE/Executive-Summary-Generations-Research.pdf.

5. Paul White, "Do Millennials Prefer to Be Shown Appreciation Differently?," *Human Resource Management International Digest* 26, no. 5 (2018): 22–26, https://doi/abs/ 10.1108/HRMID-04-2018-0065.

6. In response to the need, we created a specific version of the *Motivating By Appreciation Inventory* for remote employees. For more information: http://www.appreciationatwork .com/work-personality-test/.

CHAPTER 6: *APPRECIATION LANGUAGE #3: ACTS OF SERVICE*

1. We have developed versions of the *Motivating By Appreciation Inventory* for a variety of work settings to assist in making sure the actions within each language of appreciation are appropriate for the specific workplace. To view the versions available: http://www .appreciationatwork.com/work-personality-test/.

CHAPTER 7: *APPRECIATION LANGUAGE #4: TANGIBLE GIFTS*

1. See the article: Paul White, "Do You Have a Colleague Who Is Easily Offended?," *Appreciation at Work* (blog), July 23, 2016, http://www.appreciationatwork .com/blog/colleague-easily-offended/.

2. Paul White, "100,000 Employees Share How They Want to Be Appreciated: What Is the Primary, Secondary and Least Used Appreciation Languages," *Recognition & Engagement Excellence Essentials* 4, no. 9 (2017): 5–6, https://www.hr.com/en/magazines/recognition_ engagement_excellence_essentials/september_2017_recognition_engagement/ 100000-employees-share-how-they-want-to-be-appreci_j7bu5sub.html.

3. In some work settings, giving gifts (above a certain money limit) is not allowed. As a result, we created the versions of the *Motivating By Appreciation Inventory* for nonprofit organizations, government agencies, and military settings to address these issues. For more information: www.mbainventory.com.

4. Feel free to share your "bad gift" example by writing to us at admin@appreciationatwork.com.

CHAPTER 8: *APPRECIATION LANGUAGE #5: PHYSICAL TOUCH*

1. Langer Research, "Unwanted Sexual Advances: Not Just a Hollywood Story," *ABC News/ Washington Post* poll, 2017, http://www.langerresearch.com/wp-content/uploads/ 1192a1SexualHarassment.pdf.

2. Bryan Fuller et al., "Exploring Touch as a Positive Workplace Behavior," *Human Relations* 64, no. 2 (February 10, 2011): 231–56, https://doi.org/10.1177/0018726710377931.

3. Ibid.

4. Laura E. Marler et al., "Exploring the Role of Touch and Apologies in Forgiveness of Workplace Offenses," *Journal of Managerial Issues* 23, no. 2 (2011): 144–63. http:// www.jstor.org/stable/23209223.

5. Jonathan Levav and Jennifer J. Argo, "Physical Contact and Financial Risk Taking," *Psychological Science* 21, no. 6 (June 22, 2010): 804–10, https://doi.org/10.1177/ 0956797610369493.

CHAPTER 9: *DISCOVER YOUR PRIMARY APPRECIATION LANGUAGE: THE MBA INVENTORY*

1. Paul White, "Appreciation at Work Training and the Motivating By Appreciation Inventory: Development and Validity," *Strategic HR Review* 15, no. 1 (February 8, 2016): 20–24, https://doi.org/10.1108/SHR-11-2015-0090.

2. www.appreciationatwork.com/train.

3. Additionally, an easy introduction in story form is provided in our book: Gary Chapman, Paul White and Harold Myra, *Sync or Swim: A Fable About Workplace Communication and Coming Together in a Crisis* (Chicago: Northfield Publishing, 2014).

4. Refer to the Appreciation at Work Resources Decision Making Matrix https:// www.appreciationatwork.com/wp-content/uploads/2017/10/Decision-Chart-2017.pdf.

5. White, *The Vibrant Workplace: Overcoming the Challenges to Building a Culture of Appreciation.*

6. White, "Do You Have a Colleague Who Is Easily Offended?"

7. Go to www.mbainventory.com for more information.

CHAPTER 10: *THE DIFFERENCE BETWEEN RECOGNITION AND APPRECIATION*

1. WorldatWork, "Trends in Employee Recognition," May 2017, https://www.worldatwork .org/dA/d0815e4c41/trends-in-employee-recognition-2017.pdf.
2. Stacia Sherman Garr, "The State of Employee Recognition in 2012," Bersin & Associates, June 2012, http://go.achievers.com/rs/iloverewards/images/analytstinsights-the-state-of-employee-recognition.pdf..
3. WorldatWork, "Trends in Employee Recognition."
4. Ibid.
5. This topic is more fully discussed in Chapter 10: "Performance Issues" of Paul White, *The Vibrant Workplace: Overcoming the Challenges to Building a Culture of Appreciation* (Chicago: Northfield Publishing, 2017).
6. See chapter 9, or go to www.mbainventory.com.
7. Paul White, "How Do Employees Want to Be Shown Appreciation? Results from 100,000 Employees," Strategic HR Review 16, no. 4 (2017): 197–99, https://doi.org/10.1108/SHR-06-2017-0037.
8. Paul White, "Don't Hire Your Clones: Diversity in Practice," Human Talent Network, July 20, 2015, https://www.humantalentnetwork.com/dont-hire-your-clones-diversity-in-practice/7595/#contentanchor.
9. Leigh Branham, *The 7 Hidden Reasons Employees Leave: How to Recognize the Subtle Signs and Act Before It's Too Late* (New York: AMACOM, 2005).
10. White, "How Do Employees Want to Be Shown Appreciation?"

CHAPTER 11: *YOUR POTENTIAL BLIND SPOT: YOUR LEAST VALUED LANGUAGE*

1. SHRM/Globoforce, "SHRM/Globoforce Employee Recognition Survey," Fall 2012, http://go.globoforce.com/rs/globoforce/images/SHRMFALL2012Survey_web.pdf.
2. For more information, see the chapter on understanding others' differences in Paul White, *The Vibrant Workplace: Overcoming the Challenges to Building a Culture of Appreciation* (Chicago: Northfield Publishing, 2017).
3. Brian T. Gregory, K. Nathan Moates, and Sean T. Gregory, "An Exploration of Perspective Taking as an Antecedent of Transformational Leadership Behavior," *Leadership & Organization Development Journal* 32, no. 8 (November 12, 2011): 807–16, https://doi org/10.1108/01437731111183748.

CHAPTER 12: *APPRECIATION WITH REMOTE EMPLOYEES AND VIRTUAL TEAMS*

1. Jeffrey M. Jones, "In U.S., Telecommuting for Work Climbs to 37%," Gallup, August 19, 2015, http://news.gallup.com/poll/184649/telecommuting-work-climbs.aspx.
2. Gallup, "State of the American Workplace," 2017, http://news.gallup.com/reports/199961/7.aspx.

3. David Hassell, "Infographic: Should You Allow Remote Work At Your Company?," *15Five* (blog), 2017, http://www.15five.com/blog/infographic-should-you-allow-remote-work-at-your-
company/.
4. Gallup, "State of the American Workplace."
5. Global Workplace Analytics, "Latest Telecommuting Statistics," 2017, http:// globalworkplaceanalytics.com/telecommuting-statistics.
6. Remote.co, "10 Stats About Remote Work," October 5, 2015 (updated March, 2017), https://remote.co/10-stats-about-remote-work/.
7. CoSo, "CoSo Cloud Survey Shows Working Remotely Benefits Employers and Employees," 2017, http://www.cosocloud.com/press-release/connectsolutions-survey-shows-working-remotely-benefits-employers-and-employees.
8. Gallup, "State of the American Workplace."
9. Scott Edinger, "Why Remote Workers Are More (Yes, More) Engaged," August 24, 2012, https://hbr.org/2012/08/are-you-taking-your-people-for.
10. AfterCollege, "2015 Aftercollege Career Insight Survey," 2015, https://www.aftercollege .com/cf/2015-annual-survey.
11. www.mbainventory.com.
12. Paul White, "Appreciation with Remote Staff and Virtual Teams," September 13, 2017, http://www.appreciationatwork.com/blog/appreciation-remote-staff-virtual-teams/.
13. Paul White, "Do Remote Employees Want to Be Shown Appreciation Differently Than Employees in Face-to-Face Settings?," *Training Magazine*, October 2, 2018, https:// trainingmag.com/do-remote-employees-want-be-shown-appreciation-differently-employees-face-face-settings/.
14. This issue is addressed more fully in Paul White, *The Vibrant Workplace: Overcoming the Challenges to Building a Culture of Appreciation* (Chicago: Northfield Publishing, 2017).
15. We have created resources for virtual teams to help them apply the concepts from the *Appreciation at Work* training kit. Go to: www.appreciationatwork.com/train.

CHAPTER 13: *GENERATIONAL DIFFERENCES AND OTHER FAQS*

1. See a more thorough discussion of these generational issues in: Paul White, *The Vibrant Workplace: Overcoming the Challenges to Building a Culture of Appreciation* (Chicago: Northfield Publishing, 2017).
2. Paul White, "Do Millennials Prefer to Be Shown Appreciation Differently?," *Human Resource Management International Digest* 26, no. 5 (2018): 22–26, https://doi/abs/ 10.1108/HRMID-04-2018-0065.
3. White, "How Do Employees Want to Be Shown Appreciation? Results from 100,000 Employees."
4. Paul White, "How to Determine If Your Employees Are Burned Out," Corporate Wellness Magazine, 2017, http://www.corporatewellnessmagazine.com/mental-health/ burned-out-employees/.

CHAPTER 14: *HOW APPRECIATION WORKS IN DIFFERENT SETTINGS*

1. Go to www.mbainventory.com to learn about the different versions of the inventory, including versions for schools, government agencies, medical settings, the military, long distance work relationships, nonprofit organizations, and ministries.
2. Nona Momeni, "The Relation between Managers' Emotional Intelligence and the Organizational Climate They Create," *Public Personnel Management* 38, no. 2 (June 1, 2009): 35–48, https://doi.org/10.1177/009102600903800203.
3. Robert Roy Johnson, "Supervising with Emotion," *Law & Order* 55, no. 2 (2007): 12–14, https://www.highbeam.com/doc/1P3-1240593211.html.
4. Go to www.appreciationatwork.com/international for more information.

CHAPTER 16: *OVERCOMING YOUR CHALLENGES*

1. The issue of busyness is so critical to understand and address, we devoted a full chapter to it in White, *The Vibrant Workplace: Overcoming the Challenges to Building a Culture of Appreciation.*
2. Stephen R. Covey, A. Roger Merrill, and Rebecca R. Merrill, *First Things First: To Live, to Love, to Learn, to Leave a Legacy* (New York: Fireside, 1996).
3. Stephen Covey, *The 7 Habits of Highly Effective People Restoring the Character Ethic* (New York: Free Press, 2004).
4. Martin Dewhurst, Matthew Guthridge, and Elizabeth Mohr, "Motivating People: Getting Beyond Money."
5. Paul White, "Communicating Appreciation Effectively When You Manage Large Groups," HR.com, *Rewards & Recognition Employee Engagement Excellence* 5, no. 4 (April 4, 2018): 44–45, https://www.hr.com/en/magazines/recognition_engagement_excellence_essentials/april_2018_recognition_engagement/communicating-appreciation-effectively-when-you-ma_jfsj0tki.html.
6. Paul White, "The 5 Languages Of Appreciation In Tech: A Soft Skills Tool For Engineers," *15Five* (blog), 2017, https://www.15five.com/blog/employee-appreciation-tech-industry-engineers-soft-skills/.
7. Paul White, "Practical Ways to Show Appreciation to Colleagues in High Tech Settings," January 5, 2018, https://www.linkedin.com/pulse/practical-ways-show-appreciation-colleagues-high-tech-white-ph-d-/.

CHAPTER 17: *WHAT IF YOU DON'T APPRECIATE YOUR TEAM MEMBERS?*

1. This issue is discussed more fully in the chapter "Performance Issues" in White, *The Vibrant Workplace: Overcoming the Challenges to Building a Culture of Appreciation.*
2. See the article which explores the concept of what constitutes a "good work ethic": Paul White, "What Is a 'Good Work Ethic', Really?," Appreciation at Work Blog, 2017, http://www.appreciationatwork.com/blog/what-is-a-good-work-ethic-really/.
3. An excellent resource is: Douglas Stone, Bruce Patton, and Sheila Heen, *Difficult Conversations: How to Discuss What Matters Most* (New York: Penguin Books, 2000).

CHAPTER 18: *NOW IT'S YOUR TURN*

1. We have researched toxic workplaces and have created a number of resources to understand (and survive) them, including *Rising Above a Toxic Workplace, The Toxic Workplace Prevention and Repair Kit,* and the *Ratings of Toxic Symptoms Scale.* Go to www.appreciationatwork.com for more information.

2. For help in knowing which resources best fit your situation, see our decision-making matrix at: https://www.appreciationatwork.com/wp-content/uploads/2017/10/Decision-Chart-2017.pdf.

ABOUT THE AUTHORS

GARY CHAPMAN, PhD—author, speaker, pastor, and counselor —has a passion for people, and for helping them form lasting relationships. Chapman is a well-known marriage counselor and director of marriage seminars. *The 5 Love Languages®* is one of Chapman's most popular titles, selling over 12 million copies and topping various bestseller charts for years, including appearing on the *New York Times* bestseller list continuously since 2007. Chapman has been directly involved in real-life family counseling since the beginning of his ministry years, and his nationally syndicated radio programs air on Moody Radio Network and more than 400 affiliate stations.

For more information visit www.5lovelanguages.com.

DR. PAUL WHITE is a psychologist, speaker, and leadership trainer who "makes work relationships work." His professional focus is to provide practical, easy-to-implement resources to help leaders and organizations build healthy workplace cultures. His books and training materials have been translated into seventeen languages and used in more than sixty countries. He has consulted with multinational corporations, government agencies, medical facilities, schools, family-owned businesses, nonprofit organizations, and more.

For more information, visit www.appreciationatwork.com.

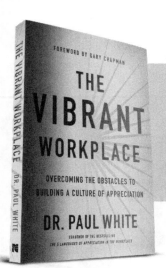

From psychologist and consultant Dr. Paul White comes *The Vibrant Workplace*, a field guide for rooting out negativity and cultivating trust in every level of your organization. Readers will learn how organizational culture works, how to facilitate systemic change over time, and why appreciation is the key to healthy teams.

978-0-8024-1503-5 | also available as an eBook

Many today are experiencing the reality of bullying bosses, poisonous people, and soul-crushing cultures on a daily basis. Insightfully illustrating from real-life stories, *Rising Above a Toxic Workplace* delivers practical hope and guidance for those who find themselves in an unhealthy work environment.

978-0-8024-0972-0 | also available as an eBook

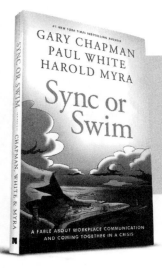

Sync or Swim is a small tale with enormous insight on ways you can empower, engage, and energize employees or volunteers facing discouragement or cynicism. Based on the principles successfully used by major corporations, health organizations, over 250 colleges and universities, government agencies, churches and non-profits.

978-0-8024-1223-2 | also available as an eBook

FOR MORE INFORMATION, VISIT
appreciationatwork.com

NORTHFIELD
PUBLISHING

Appreciation at Work™ Implementation Kit

Appreciation at Work™ Online Training Course

Become a certified facilitator and help others discover how to empower organizations by encouraging people.

IDEAL FOR:

- Supervisor or Team Leader
- Human Resource professional or internal corporate trainer
- Business or organizational coach, consultant, or trainer

FOR MORE INFORMATION ABOUT TRAINING RESOURCES, VISIT **appreciationatwork.com/train**.

Dr. Paul White
"Making Work Relationships Work."

Dr. Paul White is available for speaking and training for businesses, organizations, and associations. Please visit drpaulwhite.com to see video clips, potential topics, training resources, and other details of how Dr. White can serve your organization.